The Pirates of My Soul

of

My Soul

A Transformational Voyage
to Self-Empowerment

Kendyl Jameson

The End
Result

ISBN: 978-0-9992498-2-6 (paperback)
ISBN: 978-0-9992498-5-7 (ebook)

Library of Congress Control Number: 2021906136

First Edition

The Pirates of My Soul: A Transformational Voyage to Self-Empowerment is based on a true story. All names and identifying details have been changed to protect privacy. Business names are fictitious; any resemblance to actual businesses is coincidental.

Advice is provided without guarantee. The End Result and the author shall not be liable for any loss or damage suffered by readers as a result of any advice or suggestions contained herein.

Cover art by Kendyl Jameson.

Visit the author's website at KendylJameson.com.

Publisher's Cataloging-in-Publication data

Names: Jameson, Kendyl, author.
Title: The pirates of my soul : a transformational voyage to self-empowerment / Kendyl Jameson.
Description: Delray Beach, FL: The End Result, 2021.
Identifiers: LCCN: 2021906136 | ISBN: 978-0-9992498-2-6 (paperback) | 978-0-9992498-5-7 (ebook)
Subjects: LCSH Jameson, Kendyl. | Man-woman relationships. | Dating (Social customs) | Self-actualization (Psychology) | Interpersonal relations. | BISAC FAMILY & RELATIONSHIPS / Dating | BIOGRAPHY & AUTOBIOGRAPHY / Personal Memoirs
Classification: LCC HQ801.A2 J36 2021 | DDC 306.7--dc23

For Dad

CONTENTS

CONTENTS

Dear Reader,

Pour yourself a coffee or have a cup of tea.
　Sip, perhaps, a glass of wine as you begin to read.

My wish is that you'll enter here, feel free to come inside,
　For in my story that I tell, I've nothing left to hide.

Leave all your cares & troubles, your doubts & fears behind,
　As it is my life we review in fast rewind.

Absorb the details that you read & take what part you need
　To stop the things you see herein that cause a heart to bleed.

Sit back, but pay attention, for my tale has at its goal
　To share the lessons learned from

The Pirates of My Soul

-Kendyl Jameson

Prologue

"Honey, go tell Dad lunch is ready, please," she said to her youngest daughter.

"Okay, Mama."

The four-year-old bounced down the stairs, her blonde pigtails flying as she ran to the garage. She found her father working at his workbench and danced her way to his side. Wiggling and giggling with excitement, she tugged on his shirt.

"Daddy, Mama said lunch is ready. Come on, Daddy, it's time to eat!"

He was engrossed in the intricate work of repairing his favorite watch when he glanced in her direction. "I'll be there in a minute," he said. Dismissing his daughter, he turned his attention back to the task at hand.

"Okay, I'll tell Mama," she said, disappearing inside.

Returning to the kitchen, she joined her mother and eagerly waited. With the two older girls in school, it was only the three of them at home.

A few minutes later, her father came in and kissed his wife on the cheek. Looking over her shoulder, he inhaled deeply, savoring the smell of the cooked ham and hot, freshly buttered, homemade sweet rolls.

"Mmm, something sure smells good!"

"Yes, I know you two both love what's on the menu today," she said, nodding toward her daughter and winking at her husband. Nudging him out of the way, she set lunch on the table.

They took their seats and began passing the dishes. As they were passed to him, he prepared his daughter's plate. Sticking to his routine, he heaped the mashed potatoes and green beans onto her plate and insisted she eat all of them.

Although she hated vegetables, today was an exception because this was one of her favorite meals. However, she wouldn't get to enjoy it because there would be a twist when she took her first bite.

The mashed potatoes were covered with ham gravy and looked yummy. She took a bite of them first, anticipating a soft, creamy mouthful of warm, smooth potatoes and salty topping. But instead, they were pasty with thick, coarse strings. The strings became tangled, zigzagging back and forth inside her mouth, snaking toward her throat.

Tears formed without warning, turning her blue eyes into deep, dark pools. She tried to swallow but couldn't, unable to overcome the texture. Her throat clenched and saliva gushed in, swelling the mouthful and causing her to gag. Anxious to keep it together, she jumped up from her seat with shaking legs, fighting to postpone the inevitable.

"I have to go to the bathroom! I'm gonna throw up!"

"You aren't going anywhere," her father said. He was glaring at her, his mood instantly darkening. He pointed to the floor with several sharp jabs of his index finger. "If you need to get sick, do it right here."

Seconds later, she threw up at his feet. Vomit flowed under his chair, the potatoes creating mounds on the tile like tiny islands in a toxic, orange ocean. Terrified, she trembled as she stood before him with tears spilling down her cheeks, dreading whatever would come next.

"Now, clean that up!" he shouted.

"She will not," her mother said. "She asked to go to the bathroom. You told her to stay put, so now this is your mess. *You* clean it up!"

She tossed him a wet cloth, marking the finality of her statement. Then she turned and dried the tear-streaked face of the young girl looking up at her, calming her with soothing words.

Although her mother had defended her, the stage was set. Mealtimes would embody emotional angst, and food now held a new identity that represented something other than a means of nourishment.

Chapter 1

The Oath

I took an oath of silence and vowed to not reveal their identities. I, too often, quietly and unwittingly chose to pretend it never happened. I allowed the truth to subside into the corners of my mind where it became a mere figment, making it easier to continue.

I went through these motions countless times in an effort to regain my prize possession, the one thing no one should ever have to sacrifice to be accepted or loved by another. Every time I completed the process, I did it subconsciously and unaware of the cause of, or need for, my actions.

Throughout my experiences with the majority of these individuals, I was not allowed to have a voice. However, this is my story, not theirs, and here I do have a voice. Now, emulating those to whom I refer, those who spoke lies and practiced acts of betrayal and pure sabotage, I am doing what I want.

I am telling my tale and revealing the roles they each played. I will divulge the truth to you, sparing none, and introduce the precious secrets hidden within my treasure chest. These secrets represent both the men of whom I write, as well as the lessons learned through the temporary loss of love and self.

In fairness to all parties involved, I did not recognize the individuals described in my story as pirates until after the relationship had taken its twists and turns and the truth became clear. Although some of the men might not have been intentional with their actions, the result was the same.

As the story unfolds, you will see how each of these men gradually became the pirates of my soul, but never the captain of my heart. It is for this reason they are being held accountable herein for their attempts to destroy that which they had stolen. That, which is not spendable treasure, yet haunts all who seek to own it.

Therefore, let it be known that this prize possession, the item I have stolen back, is my soul. The absolute core of my being.

The true essence of me.

Chapter 2

Setting the Course

I know now this story's underlying theme started long before, but I think back to a moment in time when I marked my destiny for a particular course, at least geographically.

I was in seventh grade. I had been out working on the farm in one of the fields of beautiful coniferous trees all morning, and I was freezing. The day was dreary with a heavy, gray sky that, combined with the fluctuating temperature, set the tone for both the day as well as my mood.

For a while, things were tolerable while the temperature hovered around the mid-twenties. It was cold, but at least it was calm and dry. After the morning hours passed, the heat wave of the early afternoon set in and caused the temps to slide up and down the thermometer, moving continuously between freezing and slightly above.

Along with the rise in temperature came the wind that brought the precipitation, which varied between snow, sleet, and rain. Although this weather is typical for Michigan in early spring, it was dismal and depressing from any point of view, and especially mine as I toiled away.

By mid-afternoon, my gloves and coveralls were drenched, cold, and stiff. The jeans and flannel I wore underneath were sticking to me in places I didn't know existed and preferred not to think about. Soaked to the bone with numb, pruney fingers and toes, I was irritable and feeling quite ugly in general.

Hoping to improve my situation, I headed inside. I needed to take a few minutes to thaw out a bit, toss on dry duds, and grab a quick bite to eat.

Relieved to feel the warmth on my face, I peeled off the gloves and began unlacing my boots. However, before I could slip my feet out, my father walked in.

Glancing in my direction, he instructed me to go back to work immediately, making it clear I was not to question him. For some reason, the endless stream of work to be done could not wait for my physical comfort (or my crappy attitude), to be nurtured the slightest bit.

Still wet and miserable, I huffed and muttered as I laced up my boots, grabbed a clean pair of gloves, and made my way to the door. Feeling the need to emphasize my point somehow, I stomped as heavily as I could, taking advantage of the weight of my soggy boots. I was angry and I wanted the world to know.

My mind was racing with things I could not say but needed to express. Frustrated and trying to avoid verbalizing something that would bring out my father's wrath, I clenched my mouth shut. But then, as I put my hand on the doorknob and opened the door, I came up with a solution, albeit one in the distant future.

"When I'm big enough, I'm moving to *Florida*!" I yelled to anyone who might hear me, and hoping everyone would. Satisfied with my proclamation, I slammed the door behind me to seal the deal.

My announcement is funny in retrospect, because I had never been to Florida. I had only heard rumors of how warm and sunny the elusive place was from friends and relatives who had been there.

Despite my ignorance, I must have announced my intentions with enough passion to put a plan in motion. And long after my temper had cooled, my premature announcement began to make sense.

I had just turned the corner into my twenties. Watching the national weather on yet another particularly gray and unfriendly day, I realized how much warmer the weather was in Florida.

As I thought about it, I connected the dots and knew that it wasn't a rumor after all, and the flame of relocating to a warmer climate was lit.

Chapter 3

The Maiden Voyage

We met at a local sports bar when I was out with a friend, feeling frisky and flirtatious. I saw him across the room, laughing lightheartedly with his friend.

He was kicked back, his heavy work boots resting on the rung of a nearby chair. His gorgeous blue eyes made their way to mine and he smiled an easy, perfect smile. Between his cool demeanor and alluring gaze, I was hooked.

After we each shared a few exchanges with our friends and several glances passed between us, I decided to make a bold move and walked over to his table. Wearing a devilish grin and confident of a positive response, I placed one hand on the back of his chair and leaned over his shoulder, allowing my long blonde hair to tickle his neck. The smell of his well-worn, black leather greeted me like an old friend as I whispered in his ear.

"You have a beautiful smile. Do you mind if I try it on?"

Blushing and speechless, he fumbled unsuccessfully for words. Jolting upright in his seat, he almost tipped the other chair over and hastily reached out to steady it. I laughed lightly and turned to leave, brushing his shoulder with my fingertips. I had broken the ice and now the rest was up to him.

He found his feet and quickly followed, closing the gap between us. Standing 5′10″, he was slender with tussled dark hair and appeared to have personally invented the bad-boy look. His tired jeans were ripped in all the right places but his crisp, white T-shirt was tucked in nice and neat.

He came to my side and assumed a casual stance, adjusting his jacket and clearing his throat before speaking. Massaging the back of his neck with one hand, he motioned to the bar with the other.

"Can I get ya a drink?" he asked.

"Yes, thanks. I'd love a JD. Neat."

His eyebrows shot up and once again, that incredible smile appeared. "Really? Shot of Jack? Awesome." Turning toward the bar, he winked and added, "Girl after my own heart."

The night was fun, sexy, and full of flirtation. When it came to an end, we exchanged numbers and set up our first date later that week before parting ways. Soon after our first encounter, and much to my parents' dismay, I was dating Bad Boy exclusively.

Prior to meeting him, I was working full time in my first career after college and had recently bought my first home. However, shortly after our first date and within three months of that purchase, I was permanently laid off as the country began its slippery, downward slide into a recession.

A few months into the relationship, my unemployment checks ceased to arrive. Due to the depressing economy, our employment options were limited and we were both struggling to find our way. As our finances fell apart, we learned to rely on each other and, because I owned my home, he moved in with me.

Even though he was helping out, it wasn't enough and it dawned on me that I would have to sell to avoid foreclosure. Naturally, this meant moving to a new place, but where would we go?

And then I remembered how I wanted to move to Florida when I was big enough. Why not now? I wasn't being forced to stay, and nothing was holding me back.

While I thought about my situation, I looked outside. Staring out at yet another gray day, I saw my grim reality reflected in the monotony of the miserable weather. I sat immobilized, feeling the weight of the day set in.

Allowing thoughts to take their course, the details pieced themselves together. Combined, they created the perfect environment for a fantasy to spring to life. The temptation of the warm, tropical weather further south intensified, and while I pondered the idea of being surrounded by warmth every day, I realized I was in control of deciding where I lived.

I studied Florida's weather pattern for several weeks and saw that the temperatures were consistently warmer from West Palm Beach, continuing south. After this brief period of research, I knew it was the place for me.

I realized it was time to move on and right then, I made a decision that would alter the course of my life forever. At the same time, I knew I didn't want to go alone, and thought about Bad Boy.

Although we were still together, our relationship had deteriorated from flame to fizzle after the initial excitement wore off. And, even though many relationships may sever at this point, we were used to meeting our financial commitments through combined efforts. By working together, we were able to stay afloat, which had provided relief and a sense of comfort.

From that perspective and despite being more friends than lovers, I thought it would be best if we made the move together. Therefore, that evening while fixing dinner, I asked him if he wanted to go.

"Yeah, I hate this crappy weather," he said. "When were ya thinkin'?"

"How about on the first of November?"

"Good. We'll be gone before winter," he said, humming as he set the glasses on the table.

Relieved, I was pleased that he wanted to go with me. His humming confirmed his response and it was obvious we were both excited. Unable to wait, we started making our to-do lists while we ate.

The next morning, I set to work, eager to start my new life and on a self-imposed time limit. That afternoon, I listed my home with a real estate agent. Later that week, I sold my car. The following weekend, I hosted an impromptu yard sale to sell the contents of my home for moving funds. At the end of the month, we visited my family to say goodbye.

With everything in order, we packed up whatever fit in his tiny sports car and left Michigan, heading straight for West Palm Beach. Armed with a map to guide us, we would figure out the rest upon our arrival.

And so it was that my maiden voyage began, with my first pirate blissfully in tow.

Chapter 4

Coming in to Port

We arrived in Florida one bright, sunny day in November, two days after leaving Michigan. Our timing was perfect. The day before we left, an ice storm coated the roads with slick sheets of ice, confirming my rationale behind taking the giant leap into the vast unknown.

"Where are we?" I asked, waking up from a nap. We had crossed the border four hours ago and were still driving. "Man, this drive is exhausting. I can't believe I thought we'd just get in the car and *go* to Florida!"

I yawned and laughed at my own naïveté. Looking around, we took in our new surroundings and rolled down the windows. We each took a deep breath as the warm air rushed in and engulfed us.

"Well, maybe we don't know where we're at or what we're doin', but we're here," he said.

It was as though we had stepped into a whole other world. Within the span of two days, we traveled from dense gray skies, freezing temperatures, ice-covered highways and byways to dry roads without potholes, clear sunny skies, and palm trees gently swaying in the balmy breeze. It was the opposite of Michigan and we knew we had found paradise.

Clueless about where we were, we agreed any exit would suffice, as long as it was in the warmest part of the state. When we saw one for West Palm Beach, we took it, satisfied with having arrived.

We were sitting at a red light at the end of the exit ramp, when it was time to make another decision. It occurred to me that up to this point, the only thought I put into where we were heading was the name of the town and nothing more. Not one other detail was considered, but then as ignorant as we both were of Florida, I'm not sure how well any plans would have worked out.

"Okay, so, which way do we go?" he asked.

"East, to see the ocean. That's why we're here!"

The light turned green and we were on our way again. Eventually, we found the ocean and a spot with restaurants, a convenient store, and a small hotel situated within yards of the beach. Too tired to look elsewhere for a place to stay, we went in to the front desk and rented a room by the week.

Upstairs, we unlocked the door and the musty odor of our drab room welcomed us home. A quick glance around revealed an old Murphy bed, cheap, velvet art prints askew on the dingy, pale-blue walls, and two threadbare paths in the maroon shag carpet. One path led to the mini refrigerator and the other, amazingly, to a stunning, million-dollar view of the ocean.

We took inventory of the kitchenette and then left to buy groceries. After picking up a few things, we unpacked and settled in, needing to rest. I grabbed the spare blankets from the closet and we pulled down the bed, laughing as it squeaked and bounced its way to the floor.

After a nap, we decided to eat in and discovered only one burner of our two-burner stove worked. Fixing the noodles first, we ate in stages and then went for a walk on the beach.

The next day, we began the arduous tasks of searching for a job and an apartment. However, considering the era to which I refer is prior to everyone having their own cell phone, I discovered we could not land a job without a phone number, could not get a phone number without an address, and could not get the address without a job.

Meanwhile, I also received a crash course pertaining to renting an apartment. I was surprised by the steep requirements (landlords requiring first, last, and security up front), causing me to wonder how anyone could afford to move anywhere within the state.

With this discovery, I realized I had not withdrawn enough money from my bank account. Naturally, I concluded by the time we found a place where we wanted to live, our cash would be running low.

In addition, I was being denied simple work opportunities because I was over-qualified, and he wasn't scoring any better. We were both running out of ideas and, because neither of us had a work history or any personal connections in Florida, we were out of luck.

Reality struck again, shaking me out of my balmy, tropical daze as I acknowledged defeat. We were out of money and neither of us could find a job. If we did not act quickly, we would be homeless within a few days.

Cramped in the tiny hotel room, I was focusing on trying to find a solution. Leaning against the counter, I studied Bad Boy, slumped on the edge of the bed and rubbing his forehead. He appeared to be lost in thought.

"Hey, you know we need to do something fast. We're out of cash," I said, pulling the last bottle of water from the fridge and offering to share it.

"No thanks," he said, waving it away. "I know, but I don't have any more money. Brought it all."

"Well, the only thing I can do is try to cash a check. I can't believe we can't get jobs. This is such BS! I've never heard of being *over-qualified* for a simple job. What's that even about?" I asked, pacing the space of our dinky room. Now I understood why there were paths worn deep into the shag-covered floor. "Regardless of whether or not I can get any money, we need to go home. I can't support us."

"Yeah, this sucks. I don't know what else to do, either. I'll see if my brother can help when we get back."

Sadly, it had been six weeks since we arrived in Florida and now it was time to leave. We packed the car that afternoon and left the next morning.

Broke and hungry, we stopped at the gas station to fuel the car before finding something to eat. Bad Boy began filling the tank, while I ran across the street to a bank for the money we needed to pay for the gas.

"Good morning," I said, smiling as I pulled the checkbook out of my handbag and approached the counter. "I'm from Michigan and need to cash a check for $20.00, please." I found a few pieces of identification in my wallet and placed them on the counter before the teller.

"I'm sorry, but we can't cash an out-of-state check unless you have an account with us," she said.

Dismissing me without further discussion, she indicated that I should step aside. Looking past me, she motioned with her eyes for the next person to proceed to the counter.

"But wait, can't you call my bank to confirm the money is there?" I asked.

She returned my question with a firm, unforgiving expression coupled with silence while tapping her fingers on the counter. Sighing, she raised an eyebrow and looked from me to the door and back again.

I was shocked that she refused to answer my question or try to help. Frustrated, angry, and feeling helpless, I swept the pieces of identification into my bag and stepped aside. Voices swirled in muffled chaos around me while I frantically analyzed the situation.

I was hungry and desperate. Naturally, things make more sense when you are in a stable state of mind, but that morning I was not. I was aware that if we drove away from the pump without paying, we could be arrested.

This singular detail took precedence over their rules as my mind raced for a solution that would guarantee a positive result. But before I knew what I was doing, I erupted into a tantrum in the lobby.

I was creating a loud, obnoxious scene as I wailed and flailed like a wild woman. No one could ignore it, although everyone tried. I had already been dismissed, so why should I care?

I knew I would never see these people again. This fact allowed them to become insignificant and eliminated the need to be embarrassed, even though I should have been thoroughly mortified.

Meanwhile, an older, chubby man rushed across the lobby toward me in quick little steps, glancing at the tellers and shaking his nearly bald head. In hushed tones, he told me he was the manager and proceeded to explain why I could not behave like that in the bank.

Was he serious? Did he think I didn't know that already? Even though I was doing it, that didn't mean I believed it was socially acceptable, normal behavior.

However, I did not exist at that moment under normal conditions. Any and all perceptions of what should be considered normal behavior had gone out the window. New rules were being written and applied as each moment passed. I wasn't hurting anyone, nor was I committing a crime. I was merely trying to get what I needed.

Ignoring the manager's request, I persisted. When he realized his efforts were futile, he ushered me to his office where we sat and he introduced me to the rules of banking in Florida. I was nearing hyperventilation with fear of no recovery, when a teller stepped into his office.

"Excuse me," she said, handing me a twenty. "I overheard you and I've been where you're at. Please take this."

"Wow, thank you," I said, taking the money. "Let me write you a check. What's your name?"

"No, that's not necessary. I know what you're going through." Her eyes were soft and caring, and I realized she might be my only chance of getting out of Florida that morning.

"Would you trade a check for $40.00 in cash? I hate to ask, but I can't access my money here. I promise it's good."

"Sure, I'd be happy to."

She fished another bill from her purse and set it on the manager's desk in front of me. I wrote the check while he sat rigid and silent in the background, appearing bewildered and unable to comprehend the transaction taking place before him. It gave me pleasure to turn my back on him when I rose to give her the check.

We hugged as I thanked her for her generosity and compassion, and for having been my guardian angel that morning. She accepted my gratitude and wished me well on my journey.

Depleted and drained from the experience, I made my way to the exit, pleased to be armed with some money and a bit of hope for humanity. I crossed the street to join Bad Boy, who was waiting at the fueled getaway car, still parked at the pump.

After paying our bill, we headed back to I-95, back to Michigan, and back to the place I had been determined to leave.

But not without taking a local phone book with me.

Chapter 5

Retreat to Familiar Territory

After the stressful events of the morning, I settled into the passenger seat. Heading north on I-95, we began our retreat to familiar territory and prepared for the humiliating return. Frustrated, I resented that my Florida future must be put on hold, at least for now.

When we crossed the Michigan border, our attitude was deflated and similar to that of a defeated champion. From our perspective, the situation was worse now than it was before we left. It also didn't help that neither of us had a place to stay, because I had already sold my place.

As promised and to his credit, Bad Boy phoned his brother and he agreed that we could both crash there for a few weeks. Helping out with the chores around the house to pay my rent, I slept on his sofa and thanked God every night that I had a place to sleep with a roof over my head.

During this time, I chose to reflect on my predicament and how I was the one who invited the chaos into my life. It was as though I had flung open the door and yelled to the universe to bring it on—and it delivered.

At the same time, I could also justify my actions, knowing one thing had built upon the last. The domino effect was initiated when I lost my job. The demise of my finances followed, leading to the sale of my assets.

Through my review, I understood how the entire experience forced me to deal with unexpected change and to be willing to try new things.

I also realized Bad Boy and I had overcome numerous challenges, and it might have been those which kept us together. Although the romance had all but completely dissipated, we handled our situation well as we continued resolving issues as a team.

While I was pondering my reality, he discussed our predicament with his brother who told him about an opening at the auto auction. Thankful to catch a break, I seized the opportunity and began working the same week.

In the meantime, Bad Boy managed to gain a few odd jobs through his previous employer. However, the economy had not improved, making it difficult for us to patch together a paycheck. We were both doing our best to create something we could call an income, but it was not enough.

Then, one afternoon at the auction, two men approached me with a job offer. They attended weekly and although we always chatted, this time they asked if I would be interested in becoming the general manager for their dealership.

"Where are you located?" I asked.

"Twenty minutes south, in Grand Rapids," said the tall one.

"I've never been a manager, but I'm interested and a fast learner. If that's okay, I'll take the job and start working on relocating this afternoon."

"That's great," the other one replied. "We like your work ethic and how you deal with the public. We'll teach you the rest."

I thanked them for the compliment and we settled on a starting date. I was thrilled to have the new position and eager to make it come together.

Grateful for the perfect timing of an awesome opportunity, I couldn't wait to tell Bad Boy and his brother. That evening, I shared my news with them, and the two of us began working on a plan to move closer to my new job. The next day, we took a trip to scope out the area.

Luckily, we found a cute, two-bedroom apartment located near the dealership. We signed the lease and moved in the following week.

I was thrilled to be moving forward. With the details of an income and a new home in place, there remained only one more for me to settle.

We had been sharing Bad Boy's car since our move to Florida, and now I needed my own vehicle. I checked out the inventory at work and bought a car during my first week. Excited to have transportation, a place to call home, and a steady paycheck, I was determined to keep all three.

Therefore, I immersed myself in work, learning everything possible to meet my bosses' expectations. Immediately, I fell into pace and loved the job. It was a perfect fit for me and provided ample task diversification.

Aside from payroll, accounting, title work, inventory and attending auctions, I also ran errands. One of my duties required making daily deposits and transferring documents at the bank. It was during those visits that I became friends with the vice president, who quickly proved to be a helpful connection.

While I was embracing my improved situation, I knew it was time for Bad Boy to focus on his. Prior to this, we relied on each other and that was fair. But with my steady paycheck, the table had shifted. Now he was leaning solely on me, and it was taking its toll.

Two months passed and he was barely working. We hadn't discussed his situation in depth, but if he waited too long, I would be forced to bring it up. Thankfully, he hinted around about wanting to fix his mess one cloudless Sunday afternoon, while we were washing our cars.

"Kendyl, does your dealership have a cheap truck? This thing's on its last leg and it's useless for work," he said, washing the hood.

"I don't know. I'll check tomorrow. How much do you want to spend?"

He glanced in my direction and laughed nervously. Shrugging, he held out his empty hands before grabbing the hose and rinsing his car.

"Are you putting any down, or getting a loan for all of it?" I asked.

"See what ya got. Less than two grand."

"Alright, I'll let you know."

Arriving home from work the next day, I found Bad Boy in his room. I leaned in from the hall and told him we didn't have any trucks on the lot.

He stood, yawned, and stretched his arms toward the ceiling. "Okay, but I need a truck. Let's go find one."

"How are you going to pay for it? Before we waste time looking, let's figure it out."

"Fine. Here's the deal," he said. Sighing, he dropped onto the edge of his bed and leaned forward onto his forearms, wringing his hands in his lap. He stared at the floor for several minutes, before looking up at me. "I don't have any money and I've got awful credit. But I need a truck to get a job."

I mulled his situation over. I remembered how we pulled together in the past to make things work. I knew he always paid his bills, even if he cut it close at times. I also recalled how people helped me in the past and where I would be if they had not, and came up with a suggestion.

"What if I take the loan out and you make the payments? When it's paid for, I'll sign it over to you. I can go up to $2,500.00. Will that work?"

He studied me for a minute, contemplating the offer. "Yeah, I think that'd be the only way I could get it. Thanks."

"You're welcome. Now, let's go shopping," I said, smiling as I crossed the room and pulled him to his feet.

The next day, with help from my friend at the bank, we bought a truck. Later that week, he sold his car and made his first payment. He claimed to be ready to start working and appeared to be seeking employment. However, as the weeks passed, I noticed his work situation was not improving.

I became leery he wasn't trying as hard as he implied and reflected on our approach to finances. I gravitated toward creating a stable environment, much like the one in which I was raised. Bad Boy, however, was far less motivated. He preferred minimal responsibility and a care-free lifestyle.

This subject became a focal point of a conversation, during which I discovered we had conflicting goals. We were having spaghetti for dinner one night when I brought up the topic, hoping to hear that he had a plan.

"You haven't mentioned any job leads lately. Do you have an update?"

"No."

"Aren't you concerned you don't have a steady income?" I asked.

"No, I make enough to get by. Construction sucks in this weather."

"Yeah, I bet. So, why don't you look for something else?"

His eyes narrowed and his upper lip curled as he hurled his fork onto his plate. It bounced off and onto the beige carpet below, taking sauce with it when it fell. Ignoring his mess, he shoved his plate toward me.

"It's not as easy as you think, Kendyl. I don't have other skills and don't want to start with something new."

I took a deep breath. His tone was sharp and he was preparing for a fight. Whether he liked it or not, this was a discussion we had to have that was overdue. I had been patient, waiting for him to get his act together but it seemed it wouldn't happen without a nudge. Sipping my malbec, I contemplated how to proceed.

"Huh. Well, I get it. But you might need to be more flexible. You need to make money because my salary isn't enough for both of us."

"Do I give you crap about *your* job?" he shouted, still glaring at me as he banged his fists on the table. "I help with the bills and that should be good enough, so back off!"

Jumping to his feet, he thrust his chair backward, tipping it over. "I'm going for a drink," he said, snatching up his keys. Stepping over the chair, he threw the door open and stormed out, letting it slam shut behind him.

Surprised by the intensity of his reaction, I remained quiet throughout his tantrum. After he left, I cleaned up and replayed the conversation in my mind. I knew it was a stressful topic, but also knew he needed to start producing an income.

As I thought about it, I realized that whenever we discussed money in the past, we were in the same situation and neither of us could feel the other was pointing their finger. My intention had been to find a solution together, but he made it clear that he wasn't open to that idea. Now, having approached him calmly, I wondered how I could have prevented a fight.

When he returned later that evening, he went to his room and retreated into silence. For several days, he refused to speak to or acknowledge me, sending the message that certain topics were off limits.

In hindsight, I believe he noticed the differences building between us before I caught on. I also believe his attitude stemmed from my progress.

My newfound financial stability meant I no longer needed to rely on him and apparently brought out his insecurities. Therefore, he quickly mastered the tools at hand to subtly break me down to instill the same level of insecurity in me that he was experiencing.

Playing on any weaknesses he could, he used them to create a sense of need to save me from a problem he designed. He understood that as long as I needed him, or thought I did, then I would not end the relationship.

Focusing on financial priorities, I missed the signs of his controlling nature, which I realize I should have seen earlier. After all, I grew up with a father who used similar tactics to maintain unquestionable authority and control, always reminding me who was boss.

My first recollection is from when I was four years old. My siblings were at school and we were having lunch at home. The mashed potatoes were particularly stringy and the texture made it impossible to swallow them. I was struggling and started to gag.

"I have to go to the bathroom," I said. "I'm gonna throw up!"

"You aren't going anywhere," Dad said. "If you need to get sick, do it right here!"

He was glaring at me, his mood darkening with his jaw set firm. I was terrified as I stood before him.

Seconds later, I threw up at his feet, the vomit covering the floor under his chair. Instantly, tears began streaming down my cheeks while new ones formed, each chasing the others to my chin. Humiliated and trembling with fear, I waited for whatever would come next.

"Now, clean that up!" he shouted.

"She will not," Mom said. "She asked to go to the bathroom. You told her to stay put, so now this is your mess. *You* clean it up!"

She tossed him a wet cloth. Turning her back to him, she knelt and gently wiped away my tears.

The stage was set.

Food was not to be my friend, possibly ever. Many years to follow were haunted by miserable mealtime experiences, accentuated by Dad's adamant need to dictate what I would eat, how much, and when. He forced me to sit at the table alone for hours until my plate was clean, well into the night, every night.

After years of being incapable of embracing eating and postponing it for as long as I could, hypoglycemic tendencies surfaced in my teens. Fast forward to Bad Boy, and this detail would now be used as a tool to dominate and control our lingering relationship.

He discovered how to manipulate situations via my tendency toward low blood sugar. If I failed to eat within a reasonable amount of time from my last snack or meal, my mental awareness and physical strength would deteriorate. Once I was weakened by this lack of protein, he was instantly in control, and naturally became the person I relied on to pull me around.

Generally, my symptoms started with unprovoked irritability. A headache quickly followed, letting me know it was past time to eat. If not tended to, the symptoms progressed to uncontrollable physical shakes, a lack of comprehension of even the simplest statements, and eventually passing out. Although other symptoms are possible, that was the path mine would usually take as I dwindled down the spiral toward the mindless, black abyss lurking below.

Therefore, his warped exploitation of the dinner hour became a ploy to render me helpless.

It was a Friday morning and I was getting ready for work. He was sitting at the table eating breakfast, watching me pack my briefcase.

"Let's go out for dinner tonight," he said.

"That'd be nice. What time? I should be home around five thirty."

"How about six thirty?"

"Perfect. I'll have time to relax before getting ready. You pick the place and surprise me," I said with a coy wink, pulling my jacket on. We said our goodbyes and I headed out to greet the day.

Returning home that evening, I had a snack to tide me over and then ran a hot bath. I took a leisurely soak with lavender essential oil to relax and unwind. Afterward, I dressed, applied a touch of make-up and curled my hair. I was ready to leave right on time.

Bad Boy said he needed a few more minutes. Accepting his response, I sat to work on a photo project I wanted to finish.

I looked at the clock when my stomach started making a fuss and knew I needed to eat soon. I noticed it was quiet in his direction, and called out to him in the other room.

"Hey, it's six forty-five. Are you ready to go yet?"

"Not yet, I need a shower. I'll be ready in a few minutes."

I shook my head in disbelief and sighed, turning my attention back to the project. At ten past seven, I was hungry, frustrated, and impatient. I walked down the hall and pounded on his door.

"What are you doing? When will you be ready to go? I need to eat!"

"I know, I know! I'm almost ready!"

"How long will you be? If not soon, I'm going to eat here."

"No! Don't do that. I'm almost ready, I promise!"

"Well, speed it up, will you? I'm tired of waiting!" Sighing again, I rolled my eyes and returned to the table to wait. I could not believe that someone who had nothing to do all day couldn't be ready on time to go to an event that they had suggested.

At seven thirty, he appeared. "I'm ready to go," he said, sounding pleased with himself. "Come on, I'll get your purse. We need to get you something to eat."

"Ya think?" I said, casting him an even glare. Visually scanning him, I could not determine where he invested his time. He looked the same as always, dressed in a white tee and faded jeans. Too hungry and irritated to care, I chose not to ask.

By the time we arrived at the restaurant, it was a few minutes before eight o'clock. Upon our arrival, he saw that my condition had deteriorated and I was shaking. Listless and fading in and out mentally, I was near passing out. Interpreting this familiar phase correctly, he used it as his cue and reached out to grab the nearest server.

"Excuse me! My girlfriend's sugar has dropped and she needs to eat immediately. Please get some crackers or orange juice," he said. Turning his attention back to me, he reached across the table and stroked my hand.

The server acquiesced, returning with crackers and a small glass of juice. Placing them on the table before me, she took our order.

Bad Boy ordered for both of us, while I sat limp and disoriented. He continued to pet my hand, cooing reassuring words and apologizing for our tardy dinner hour until the server returned with the appetizers.

He appeared to revel in his award-winning performance for all who watched, convincing everyone he was there to protect me from a dreadful fate. By rendering me helpless, he created the opportunity to shine brightly in the eyes of those who dared to behold such a glimmering sight, neatly portraying himself as the hero.

His strategy worked a few times. Then, one night before the side effects kicked in, I realized this was a game to him. My health was being used as a tool to weaken me and strengthen him, creating a false sense of need, much like a state of codependency.

This is one example of how he operated that revealed his character. He used my health against me, proving he would disregard any boundaries to get what he wanted. I see now how he was successful, because it was that false sense of need creating a level of fear, which caused me to believe I could not function without him.

Is it true that I needed him to function? No, but that was what he wanted me to believe, and he was determined to make it my truth.

I will admit that I hadn't dated anyone like him before and was naïve about how his insecurities could be driving his actions. Because of this, he was able to infiltrate my self-confidence, injecting self-doubt and confusion where previously there was none. And although I knew I was not quite myself, I remained oblivious to what was going on.

As inexperienced as I was, it would be a while before I solved the mystery, discovered how he worked, and understood how his actions were affecting me. Therefore, we continued on while he contributed *just enough* to stay in the game.

Meanwhile, I looked around again and saw gray skies and gray roads providing gloomy surroundings. It looked the same as when I first fled to Florida, leaving the dismal imagery behind.

It was as though nothing had changed. My previous departure did not produce tangible results, and I believed nothing was materializing from my return to Michigan, except for an income.

I was stuck in a gray maze and couldn't find my way out.

Even though winter had turned the corner out of sight, I knew how soon it would return. Once again, my desire to move to a warmer climate was rekindled and I knew I was ready to make the change.

Remember the phone book?

I cracked it open and flipped to the apartment section, determined to contact the complex I found the previous year. It was time to plan the move back to Florida and I wanted to ensure this move would be successful.

Via multiple phone calls, I managed to set up an apartment in West Palm Beach and acquire my new address. Now, I had an actual destination with directions and a move-in date.

After settling on my new place down south, I submitted my two-week notice. I thanked my employers for the opportunity of the past year's employment and visited the bank. I knew I would miss my new friends, but as we said goodbye, we agreed to stay in touch.

I was leaving again like the first time, without hesitation and without cause for regret. For me, this was personal. I was on a mission toward the rest of my life and had to start immediately.

And so it was: goodbye Michigan, hello Florida. Again.

And of course, lacking better judgment, Bad Boy was still in tow.

Chapter 6

Return Voyage

Reflecting on this second journey, I can see how the decision to take him with me appears irrational after the way things were going. I think I subconsciously chose to ignore his irresponsible behavior and controlling nature to have someone with whom to take this great leap. Although the first move was unsuccessful, we had survived it together, and this provided a sense of safety and comfort.

Therefore, two days after leaving Michigan, we arrived together at the apartment in Florida. I took a job waitressing for fast, easy cash to maintain my new address. However, he had become used to working only when it suited him, and now appeared unconcerned with his financial situation.

Time passed and his presence, combined with his lack of desire to produce an income, became burdensome. I was contemplating telling him to move out because it was clear we were following different financial paths and they were never going to meet.

Apparently having read my mind, he sprung to life, contributing *just enough* (again) to the expenses to show effort. Truthfully, as complacency often dictates, it was easier to put up with him than to look for a new roommate to take his place. Therefore, happy to have the help, I postponed my decision and we continued on.

Consequently, because we coexisted within the same space yet rarely spoke to each other, the opportunity for romance was waiting around the corner.

I was working at the bar one night, when a handsome young man from New York sat in my section. His seductive, faded-denim-blue eyes were fixed on me the moment I approached his group, and I knew it was going to be an interesting evening.

He didn't waste any time, flirting and making me laugh with his dry, sarcastic humor during my first visit to his table. Using my quick wit, we bantered back and forth throughout the evening and when he blushed, his eyes twinkled. He appeared to enjoy the challenge I presented, and before the night came to a close, he asked me to dinner.

When we met out for our first date, I was surprised at how tall he was as he towered over me. Even though I was wearing five-inch stilettos, I felt petite and delicate next to his muscular build reaching up to 6'4".

He looked good, even better than the night we met. Maybe it was because this time he hadn't been out with the guys all night. I wasn't sure, but whatever it was, he was something to admire and I was distracted.

I was lost in thought, thinking about running my fingers through his silky black hair. It was casual but striking against the white, button-down shirt and khaki chinos, giving his appearance an easy, movie-star quality. Mildly hypnotized, I had to force myself to focus when he spoke.

After I tuned in, our date was fantastic. We went to dinner and talked and laughed for hours. It was obvious we had a connection beyond physical attraction and I embraced it, excited to see where it would lead.

When the evening came to a close and he asked me out again, I told him about my roommate to avoid rude surprises. He was undeterred and I was thrilled. After a few dates, we were dating each other exclusively.

Our relationship was filled with long talks speckled with rib-splitting laughter, spending time with friends, going out to dinner, playing racquetball, and other miscellaneous activities. There was only one topic on which we did not connect, and it was golf.

He was a professional golfer with an amazing drive (hence his nickname, Driver), and the sport was a major part of his social life. I knew he loved the game and wanted to be able to play with him occasionally, but had never touched a club. One night at dinner, I brought the topic up.

"Driver, will you teach me how to play golf, please? I want to be able to play with you once in a while."

"No. It's too hard to teach a girlfriend how to play a sport."

"How do you know what kind of pupil I'd make? You haven't tried to teach me anything yet," I said, taking a bite of the mouth-watering filet mignon. It was tender and melted in my mouth as I savored its perfection.

"Because. I tried teaching my ex," he said, sawing away at his steak.

"Huh. So, because that didn't work, you're tossing me into the same category with her," I said, reaching for my wine. "Thanks a lot. Golf is the one thing I can't do and it's everywhere. And, because I know nothing about it, I can't relate to it with you in conversation, either."

"Kendyl, it'll be easier on us if we keep it separate. Let's just enjoy everything else, and allow this to be my work," he said, moving on to his salad. He appeared to have given up on his steak for the time being.

"I respect keeping things separate in some cases, but this is different. I'm not asking to play with you all the time, but I feel disconnected when you guys talk about it. I won't argue with you because it's your work, but I will find someone else to teach me, so I don't feel like such a misfit."

His tone and body language softened as he set his fork down and took my hand in his. Gazing into my eyes, he sighed and smiled, drawing me in. However, rather than submitting to my pleas like I had hoped, he offered a weak piece of consolation.

"*You* could never be a misfit."

With that, we had both stated our case and the conversation came to a close. I was disappointed, but tried to see it from his point of view. In the meantime, this would have to suffice because I enjoyed being with him too much to let it become an issue.

When spring arrived, he mentioned his return to New York for work. We were sitting at his dining room table, discussing the rapidly approaching next few months.

"I knew you'd have to go, but I never promised to like it," I said, pushing my lips into a pout. "How do you plan to make this up to me?"

"Well, I can start by taking you to dinner tonight, then to the beach for a walk, and back here for a bit of TLC," he said, smiling mischievously.

"That's it? What am I, your dog? You're getting ready to leave for the summer and the best you've got to offer is dinner, sandy feet, and a couple of kisses? Please tell me you have a better plan than that," I said, laughing lightly while rising from my seat and moving toward him.

Standing over his seated position, I ran my fingers through his perfect hair at the base of his neck. Grabbing a soft, silky section, I pulled his head back with mock force. Our eyes locked together and I allowed my hair to tumble around us, shrouding our faces to isolate the moment.

Holding his gaze, I delicately tickled his upper lip with my tongue. Teasing him slowly with soft, full kisses, I swung one leg over his lap and moved into his space, pinning him to his chair.

After a few minutes of passionate kissing, I pulled back and lingered, thoroughly enjoying his expression. He was blushing and grinning as wide as the ocean is deep.

"I have to admit, you have unique negotiating skills," he said, wrapping his arms around me and squeezing. "I think you could ask for anything and I'd be too happy to make it happen."

"Finally! It's about time you came around to my way of thinking. What about when you're there? Will you fly me up for some weekends? I would love to see where you live and work. What do you think?"

He laughed at the lighthearted interrogation. Brushing my hair back behind my shoulder, he looked at me intently for a long moment.

"Yes, I want you to come, but you can't stay with me. There's no room, so I have to figure it out. But you have to be there for the fourth of July. We have a huge party and I know you'll love it."

"That sounds awesome! I can work with that for starters, but I don't think I should have to wait until I have sandy feet for a little TLC." Feeling playful, I slid off his lap and whispered in his ear. "I think you should work that detail out right now, confirming our agreement."

Then, allowing my fingers to slide leisurely across the top of his shoulders, I turned and strolled away. Looking back, I made sure he was following as I headed for the bedroom.

Chapter 7

A Lassie's Adventure

April arrived and true to his word, Driver packed up and headed north. It was the beginning of June when we had been separated for two months. We were getting along great, but the distance was wearing on me.

I was becoming restless and my first visit was still a month away, scheduled for the first of July. We were talking on the phone one evening, when I told him the distance bothered me.

"What do you think about me coming to New York for the summer?" I asked. "I can get a job and we'd be able to see each other."

"That's a great idea. But you know you can't stay with me. Are you okay with that?"

"Sure, it'll add to the adventure!"

"I can't make any promises, but let me ask around and see if anyone has a room to rent."

After discussing a few more details, we said goodnight. I was pleased he wanted me there and excited about the possibilities. I started planning my next move and before the end of the week, he found a room for rent in town. The next day, I told Bad Boy I was going to New York for the summer and confirmed he wanted to stay on, maintaining his share of the bills.

Although we had little to do with each other, he was a paying roommate. In addition, he had proven to be trustworthy with material things, making my decision easy. I was comfortable with the arrangement and continued with my preparations to leave.

I packed whatever I could not live without and possibly a few extras and said goodbye to my friends. I was crazy about Driver and excited to embrace a new opportunity. It was time to move on.

Settling into the driver's seat, I selected a favorite CD to set the pace, cranked the volume, and sang along like I belonged on a stage. On I-95 and heading north once again, I shifted into fifth gear and set the cruise control. Eager to see a new place and be with my new beau, I was ready for the drive ahead.

I knew I was setting off on another unpredictable escapade, making changes to my life without any promises. But that was irrelevant. I wasn't concerned about the level of commitment in the relationship. Instead, I was acting on a desire to give us a fair chance by closing the proximity gap.

Upon my arrival, Driver welcomed me with enthusiasm. He introduced me to his friends and then we drove to town to meet the couple from whom I would be renting.

As we drove up the tree-lined driveway, he pointed out the attached, four-car garage and told me to park in front of it. The house was a sprawling ranch surrounded by a three-acre lawn, nestled in amongst the trees. The gardens were amazing, and there was a waterfall at the front entrance that created a soothing ambiance as we approached and rang the bell.

The couple was welcoming and friendly as they ushered us in, offering snacks and coffee before starting the tour. After they showed us to my accommodations, they left us to unpack and settle me in.

We were impressed as we looked around. Standing in the doorway, I embraced the differences between this place and my first room in Florida. The suite was in a class of its own, elegantly furnished in rich, warm tones and appearing to go on forever.

Moving about, we took inventory of my new room, which extended out from the rear of the house and faced the woods. On one wall, the French doors opened to greet the impressive swimming pool situated within the sunken terrace, framed by spectacular gardens. Stunning floor-to-ceiling windows graced another wall, allowing natural light to flood the room and provide a cozy warmth, nudging me to move in and explore.

Peeking into the walk-in closet, I laughed at how my possessions would be swallowed up inside the space, which could house a mid-sized kitchen. I figured the granite-topped island in the middle would suffice as plenty of storage for my things, and moved on to the bathroom.

I knew this would become my private haven as soon as I saw the jetted tub seated between the double vanity and huge multi-head shower. The luxurious towels were plush and new, and the marble floors complemented the granite used throughout, creating an inviting environment.

"This suite is spectacular," I said, walking into the bedroom. I turned and swept my arms around before falling onto the king canopy bed. Throwing my arms above my head, I attempted to cover the width of the massive mattress. "I wish I could linger here without ever having to leave! This bed will be hard to get out of in the morning . . ."

"I know, I'm jealous," he said, sitting on the bed and bouncing to test its level of comfort. "Wow, that's nice. And the TV is bigger than the one in my apartment."

"Maybe you can come over and watch a movie or two, if you promise to behave," I said with a wink. Sitting up, I tickled his knee and pointed to the bay window. "Oh, and I love the window seat. If it's a rainy day, that's where I'll be, snuggled up with a book."

"Yeah, you struck it rich! Let's get you unpacked before they change their minds," he said, laughing as he stood and pulled me to my feet.

After I settled in, I began searching for work. It was difficult, though, because I wanted the lifestyle of leisure to enjoy my new surroundings. However, I had to work to pay my rent, so I considered my options.

I was tired of waiting tables and wanted to try something that could provide desirable skills. Having previously worked in an office, I decided to explore the possibility of becoming an office temp.

Prior to this moment, I had never considered it. However, the flexibility allowed with temp work promised to be an ideal match for my new lifestyle. Luckily, I found a first-rate temp agency and started working a week after arriving. Due to the variety of assignments over the summer months, I would learn valuable skills and loved the entire set up.

Meanwhile, Driver and I spent our evenings together and occasionally went to dinner with his clients. He was an exceptional golfer and quite charming, which enticed several couples to invite us to dinner and schmooze for golf tips.

I always looked forward to the evenings out, until one evening when I was surprised by how uneasy I felt afterward. I wanted to understand what had thrown me off as I reflected on the event. From my perspective, the dinner went smoothly and the two of us were getting along beautifully. But something nagged at me.

What was I missing? I had to know because it was interfering with my enthusiasm to participate. Over the next dinner, however, I would have my answer.

Four of us were enjoying conversation and incredible food at another fabulous restaurant, when the topic changed. As discreetly as possible, yet right on cue, the couple hinted around at how to perfect their strokes, lower their scores, read the greens, and improve their short games. Driver, smooth as always, responded politely and joked amiably while everyone discussed their handicaps and hang-ups with the game.

"You know, if you're willing, we'd love to play golf with the two of you sometime," the husband said. "It'd be a great way to learn new tips and get to know both of you better."

"Yes it would, but she doesn't play golf," Driver said, tilting his head in my direction.

"Why not? Don't you want to play?" they asked in unison.

"No, she doesn't," he said, smiling slightly and taking my hand in his.

A hush followed. Confused glances passed between them while I realized what was happening. They were also thrown by this tidbit, but resumed conversation with him, avoiding eye contact with me. It felt like an eternity before the evening came to a cordial close.

The truth was that I did want to learn and knew the topic would persist when we were together. Therefore, because I needed to be informed and he refused to teach me, I took matters into my own hands. Two days later, I accepted an offer of lessons from one of the other pros.

Unfortunately, when Driver caught wind of the arrangement, he told his friends to back off. I'm still foggy about why it bothered him, though, because we were not disrupting his agenda. He made it clear he did not want to teach me, and I had respected his decision.

His controlling actions were uncalled for and I felt snubbed and socially thwarted by his interference. This being the case, the next time one of the lovely couples asked us to play a round of golf and he told them of my lack of interest, I stepped up.

Looking graciously at him, I placed a loving hand on his shoulder, imitating his tender touch from the previous event. I then turned my attention to the couple and responded with as much sweetness as I could muster.

"No, it isn't that I don't want to play golf. Driver refuses to teach me, and doesn't want the other pros to teach me either. In fact, they were working with me and he told them to stop. Isn't that right, sweetie?"

The question lingered unanswered. I smiled softly, tilted my head, and gazed evenly at him, waiting for him to challenge the facts. He flushed to an intense shade of red, glaring silently at me while clenching his jaw.

He was clutching his napkin with one hand, while under the table, he squeezed my thigh tightly with the other. I raised an eyebrow to question whether or not he wanted the situation to escalate and he loosened his grip. I could see how hard he was struggling as he resisted the urge to argue.

However, these people were his bread and butter and he could not afford a scene. And after a long moment, they saved him by graciously moving on from the topic.

But he deserved being called out. He had put me in predicaments on several occasions, making statements about me in settings where I would appear temperamental if I defended myself, and now it was his turn.

I knew he would continue omitting me from his preferred activity, but that did not permit him to misrepresent me or speak condescendingly toward me. Even still, the rest of the evening passed by in a blur and afterward, heated words were exchanged.

Collectively, this was my first red flag. We were doing well otherwise, and taking everything into consideration, I chalked it up to his need to keep some of his personal life separate from his professional one.

We continued dating throughout the summer. Meanwhile, I periodi-
cally sought an update on the status of things in Florida. One afternoon, I
called my friend and neighbor to check on the apartment.

"Hey Skye, this is Kendyl. How's everything going down there?"

"Oh! I'm so glad you called. You're never going to believe this, but
the other night there was a fight in the courtyard and the police were called.
The worst part is that Bad Boy was the instigator!"

"You're kidding," I said, rolling my eyes and sighing. I couldn't tell
if she was exaggerating because she was known for getting excited about
everything. "Was anyone hurt? How bad was it?"

"No, thank goodness, but it was still nasty. We haven't heard a peep
out of him since, but I know he's around because his truck has moved.
Kendyl, can you trust him? Will he destroy the place or do anything to
your stuff?"

"Well, I'm not worried about my stuff, but I am concerned about the
apartment," I said, flicking the top of a pen while processing her news.
"I'm going to check around and see what else is going on."

The conversation continued while she provided more details. Before
it was over, I was convinced that my absence was presenting unnecessary
opportunities for problems to evolve into major issues.

"None of this sounds good," I said. "Obviously, I need to return before
anything else happens."

"If you do, let me know when you're here and make sure you take
someone with you to the apartment. It's too bad you have to come back
early, but it'll be nice to see you."

"Will do, and thanks, Skye. I'll see you soon."

I was only mildly surprised with her update. Even though he never
raised a hand to me, I witnessed Bad Boy's temper with other men while
we dated. Regardless of his ongoing social behavior, our conversation
sparked the need for me to take action.

After that call, I checked in with the leasing office and a few other
places for details pertaining to our combined financial matters. The leasing

office was aware of the fight, but stressed minimal concern pertaining to his behavior going forward.

When I contacted the bank, I discovered he was two months behind on his truck payments. I guess he kept the notices, because I never received them. This was another issue because the loan, like the apartment, was still in my name.

Throughout my research, other delinquencies were uncovered, and I knew I had to step in and take control. Adding the details together, it was clear I had to make an important decision, now considerably overdue.

I needed to evict Bad Boy.

I had moved on and knew he would not be a part of my life again. It was time to wrap things up with him.

However, after my recent discoveries, I was hesitant to return to the apartment alone. Heeding Skye's warning, I shared my concern with Driver and he agreed with her suggestion.

That evening, he called a friend in Fort Lauderdale and asked him to help me. Thanks to that phone call, I now had a bodyguard.

During the next few days, I finalized my battle plan and packed my belongings. After saying my goodbyes, I loaded the car and closed the door on the beautiful suite I was happy to call home for the past three months.

As I walked to my car that morning to head out, I wasn't sure what to expect for my immediate future. All I knew was that I needed to close a few more doors if I wanted to move forward.

Sliding in behind the wheel, I took comfort in my decision to eliminate some stress as I started the car and rolled down the driveway. Looking in the rearview mirror, it felt like I was leaving safety behind as I turned left and headed for the highway.

I drove to I-95 and took the ramp heading south. Settling in, I set my sights on West Palm Beach, Florida.

Yet again.

Chapter 8

Take No Prisoners

I informed Driver's buddy of my mission's details before he signed on. I explained how I intended to accomplish the eviction and the date of my return to West Palm Beach. I worked out the details in advance, but needed his assistance to carry it off. With a bit of luck and excellent timing, we would have this matter cleared up with minimal effort.

My unofficial bodyguard met me at the leasing office upon my arrival. He was huge and towered over me. Standing 6′5″ and weighing in easily around 280 pounds, I knew I was in good hands. No one would be dumb enough to start a fight with this guy, not even Bad Boy. He might be angry enough to explode at any given moment, but checked in at only 5′10″ and 165 pounds.

"Nice to meet you," I said, shaking his hand. It felt like I was shaking a tree trunk. "Thanks for taking time to help me with this mess. It means a lot to me."

"It's cool. I love this kinda thing and was doin' nothin'. What's next?" he asked, grinning and wringing his hands with excitement.

"First, we're going to have the locks changed," I said, indicating the leasing office and heading toward it. "I don't know if he's there, so we'll have security go with us. We'll take it as it comes after that."

I was relieved he was genuinely excited to help. I felt uncomfortable imposing on a stranger for such a huge favor and now that I was back, the depth of the situation was setting in. I was mentally gearing up for action and wanted this to be quick and easy, hoping my plan's execution would be flawless.

We went into the office where I introduced myself to the receptionist and provided a brief summary of my visit. I asked for security to escort us to my place, explaining that I had discussed this with the office during previous phone conversations. The security guard promptly accompanied us to the apartment, fully prepared for any action that might ensue.

Upon entering, there was only a young lady sitting at the counter in the kitchen. She was reading a magazine while waiting for the laundry and barely acknowledged having heard us walk in. When she glanced in my direction, I nodded toward the door.

"Do you see that door?" I asked. "Use it as an exit. Now."

She rose, gathered a few things and left peacefully. I think she knew it was only a matter of time before something like this would happen. After she left, it was time to prepare for his return.

I went to work while the locks were being changed, despite being worn out from the exhausting drive. I needed the element of surprise to reclaim the apartment without incident, and wanted to be ready when he came home.

I expected him to arrive later in the afternoon, and knew he would be furious when he discovered he was locked out. Although he should have anticipated his financial obligations to catch up with him, I doubt he suspected I would return from New York to bring them to his doorstep.

As for the truck, I needed to take possession and sell it before I could clear the debt. However, I knew my hands were tied as long as there was a lien on it.

Therefore, prior to leaving New York, I contacted my friend, the vice president, and discussed the issue. I required another favor to complete the mission, and he was the man for the job.

After explaining the situation, I asked if he would release the lien on the truck to sell it. When it sold, I would remit the funds owed to settle the debt. Even though Bad Boy was supposed to be making the payments, he knew it was my name on the loan, which was why I asked him to trust me with the entire transaction.

He agreed to my request and cleared the lien. His prompt assistance paved the way for me to fully execute my plan and I knew that without both his help, as well as that of my bodyguard, the entire feat would not be a success. Now, with everything in place, I was ready to proceed.

While preparing for the events to kick off that evening, I took inventory of the apartment. When I entered the kitchen, I saw a large set of scales. This was not a typical household set of scales and it looked out of place. I took a closer look, my curiosity piqued.

I have never indulged in or been involved with illegal drugs. But even I had seen enough movies and been to my share of parties to avoid total ignorance. These scales, perched conspicuously on the counter, had traces of an illegal substance on them. It was just enough for me to recognize, as I rubbed the white powder onto my gums.

This new tidbit made me wonder what went on during my absence. While in New York, I had reflected on the relationship and why I had kept him in my life. I acknowledged my denial of the truth about him and was disappointed in myself for allowing him to become a roommate.

However, this discovery brought everything to a new level.

Forced to admit the situation was worse than anticipated, I quietly hoped my strong attitude and huge bodyguard would be enough to quell what was certain to erupt. I needed Bad Boy to leave without creating problems, despite how much he owed.

My bodyguard was preoccupied with less demanding things as he sat watching TV, and I was too tired to worry about any of it. I gathered Bad Boy's belongings, tossing everything together into huge garbage bags and eliminating the need for him to set foot inside. Afterward, we ate sandwiches for a late lunch and waited for his return.

While waiting, I decided to call Skye and let her know I was in town. I left a message telling her I would be evicting Bad Boy that evening, but not to worry, because a friend was staying with me. I thanked her for tipping me off, and suggested we meet for coffee the following week.

A few hours later, Bad Boy arrived and tried to unlock the door. By the time I opened it, the cursing was flowing freely. He glared at me and struggled for his mental footing, unable to hide his surprise.

"What the hell?"

"Uh uh," I said, holding a hand up to stop him when he started to move forward. Before he could react, I pushed the bags through the doorway toward his feet. They hit the wooden landing beyond the threshold with a thud. "Here's your stuff; please leave. I don't want the money you owe. Just go."

"No way!" he yelled. "I'm not goin' anywhere! *I live here, you bitch!*"

"Not anymore!" I shouted back.

"Yes I do!" He lunged toward the door, trying to catch its edge above the doorknob to open it further. Stumbling over the heavy bags at his feet, he was unable to get a good grip and almost fell on his stuff. "You can't kick me out, I'm on the lease, damn it!"

"Yes I can, and I am. You haven't paid your bills," I said, pulling the door closer. "You're listed as a roommate. I don't have to let you in if you've got your stuff, and you do."

Right on cue, the large, dominating bodyguard moved into view. He leaned nonchalantly against the wall, folded his arms across his chest, and made eye contact with Bad Boy. He didn't say a word, but then, he didn't have to.

"Oh, I get it," he said, snorting as he sized up the bodyguard. Narrowing his eyes, he stared at me with contempt as he flipped his hand in the bodyguard's direction. "You thought you'd threaten me with this guy, huh?"

"No," I said, becoming impatient with his drama. "But you brought this on yourself. It's over. Goodbye, Bad Boy."

"He don't scare me! I'll be back for you and I'm gonna—"

I slammed the door, shutting him out of my life. He continued shouting nasty threats for a while and then left, temporarily accepting defeat.

Relieved to have the first part of the process under way, I thanked my bodyguard for doing exactly what needed to be done, and set off to finish the chores for the evening. I replayed the scene and thought about how lucky I was to have his assistance, knowing this was only the beginning.

Bad Boy was a man who became mean and violent when he did not get his way. He was furious to have been displaced, certainly, but by me? That was incomprehensible. He would be determined to have the last word or course of action and was bound to return.

And he did.

Night after night, he reappeared and camped out shamelessly on the doorstep. Sometimes he would loiter peacefully, hoping for the door to open, while other times I swear he could be heard all over the county, shouting threats littered with profanity.

On the nights when he sat silently stalking the front door, Skye (or one of the other neighbors who knew about the fight), would call and warn me. They were concerned for my safety and offered to call the police if I felt the need. It was apparent to everyone he was like a raging bull, foaming at the mouth and begging for a fight.

Despite his attempts to get a rise out of me, I refused to acknowledge or speak to him. I had stated my case and explained the situation to him, leaving no loose ends. There was nothing left to discuss. The facts were what they were, and trying to reason with him would be futile.

When I called the leasing office and asked if they could do anything about him occupying the front stoop at night, their suggestion was to call the police. I weighed the pros and cons. I decided it wasn't worth the risk of creating more animosity, feeling confident the situation would resolve itself in a few days.

I knew he would not be homeless for long and assumed he was already crashing on someone's sofa. I also knew his fuss was not about a roof over his head. He was furious I ambushed him and kicked him out. That was what ground his gears, even if it was deserved.

Even though he was unaware, I knew he would be moving into his new apartment in a few days. And, unfortunately, it was only two buildings from my place. I was aware of this arrangement prior to returning, which served as the prime motivator for the timing of my arrival.

You see, that is why I was able to give him everything without any mention of the truck, allowing him to keep it. I knew we would be sharing a parking lot for another week. Until, of course, he no longer had a vehicle to park there.

Fortunately, I was smart enough to have an additional key made for the truck when we bought it. I had kept it without his knowledge in case I needed it, and now it was time to put it to use.

In addition, and in the midst of everything, it did not escape my attention that the leasing office was allowing him to move next door. While in New York, I spoke to them about Bad Boy's fighting for which the police were called, stressing a concern for my safety upon my return.

Although they were cooperative in changing the locks, I doubt they had a clue that I knew where he was moving to. They were also aware of his recent threats against me.

Yet here they were, breaching their own contract by allowing him to live two buildings away. He would be living inside the gated community, maintaining full, easy access to me with his new place situated within view of my patio.

My bodyguard was a borrowed safety net and I needed to be able to protect myself after his departure. Focusing on my own welfare, I knew it was time to implement the rest of my plan.

Even though I am not someone who seeks revenge, I will defend myself when a situation such as this develops. With this clarification in mind, you will understand what we did next.

On a glorious summer evening (after Bad Boy moved into his new apartment, but before my bodyguard left), we took the truck. We stashed it far enough away from the complex that he would never find it, yet in full view of the public.

We placed the sale signs in the windows, locked it, and gave each other a high five for escaping the lot undetected. Giggling, we ran to my car and jumped in. After taking a few deep breaths to calm our adrenaline rush, we decided to go out to eat before calling it a night.

Of course, Bad Boy freaked out when he discovered the truck was gone and returned to my front door slinging more vicious verbal assaults. But again, I refused to respond. Thankfully, my bodyguard continued to make his presence known and Bad Boy refrained from any further action.

As for the truck, it sold two days later. The debt was paid, my name was cleared, and all ties to Bad Boy were officially severed.

For my safety and peace of mind, I packed and left the apartment, terminating my lease. It was the final piece necessary to eliminate Bad Boy's access to me forever, and I literally felt free.

My bodyguard helped me move into my new place before returning to Fort Lauderdale. He was my protector for two weeks throughout the mess, and now it was over. I know I would not have made it through this process smoothly without his assistance, and will always be grateful.

This part of my life reached its conclusion and I could finally breathe with ease. I never saw Bad Boy again. Nor have I seen his set of scales, for that matter.

To Bad Boy, I say thank you for the ride!

Thank you for showing me what my life would be like if I stayed with a man who left the heavy lifting to me.

Thank you for proving to me that nothing was sacred, not even my health, when it came to you getting what you want. And, even though my parents could have told me, thank you for teaching me that a *bad boy* is not harmonious with what I need or want.

Although I thank you for the lessons you taught me, I do not wish for our paths to ever cross again.

Chapter 9

Damsel in Distress

Meanwhile, Driver was still in New York. I thought about the gravity of the situation and wished the man who claimed to love me at least *acted* like he could be the one present to help me, rather than his friend. I knew his personal obligations took priority over my silly drama, but he seemed indifferent.

I confess I do not make a great damsel in distress like those who have the innate ability to make a room full of men rush, stumbling over themselves, to come to their aid over a hangnail. Instead, when I ask for help, the men in my life do not appear concerned with my well-being. It has always been more of a passing disinterest for most of them.

Please do not misunderstand me. I know they do care about me to a degree. This observation pertains in general to the lack of desire shown for direct involvement in assisting with my issue, whatever it may be.

That thought aside, my gratitude persists for Driver's introduction to his friend and the tremendous amount of help he provided in my time of need. Collectively, the assistance received by those involved (directly or indirectly), allowed me to move forward with my life. Without each one and the part they played, who knows how it would have unfolded.

On that note, having learned an important lesson from the experience with Bad Boy, my new apartment was listed in my name only. Summer ended, fall returned, and Driver eventually joined me.

As we settled in together, I thought we were enjoying our time as a couple, but something felt off. Given the time apart, we should have been cozier than we were and naturally, I began questioning our status.

By then, we had plans to spend Christmas with my family. When we flew to Michigan, my parents met us at the airport. We stopped for lunch on the way home and were discussing random topics, when Driver mentioned the two of us playing racquetball.

"She's not much of a player. She doesn't like to keep score."

"I love to play for the fun of it," I said. "It's a great form of exercise. Keeping score brings pause to the game, and I'd rather keep moving."

"Well, you have a lot of room for improvement. I don't see any point in playing, if you don't keep score. But then, that's *you*," he said, adding a forced laugh.

Silenced by the slam, I was unable to respond. Thankfully, Dad could, and he was not impressed. He put his fork down, sat back, and folded his arms.

"What *do* you like about my daughter?" he asked, looking evenly at Driver.

I was surprised Dad came to my defense, possibly for the first time ever. His inquiry hung in the open air, remaining unanswered as Driver shifted in his seat, his face instantly flushing. The mood remained tense until Mom delicately changed the topic to encourage pleasantries.

The comment was mentally noted and another red flag confirmed. I had been wondering if I was overanalyzing recent statements, but now I knew it was not my imagination. He was definitely belittling me and was comfortable doing it in front of anyone, while disguising it as an attempt at some kind of humor.

After his run-in with Dad and during our visit, he was on his best behavior. The holiday came and went without any other incidents. But when we returned to Florida, he picked up where he left off.

I paid attention to how he treated me all winter and concluded that I was supposed to be silent decoration. In addition, I thought that as a couple, we would do things together we both enjoyed, sharing our interests. However, this was also missing.

His halfhearted efforts toward our relationship were declining while he remained adamant about excluding me from the golf segment of his life. As time progressed, it became necessary to focus on his actions toward me as well as intentions with me, rather than float along.

He returned to New York in the spring and went back to work. Based on my recent observations, I decided to stay put that summer. I fine-tuned my listening skills, paying close attention to the details of our conversations.

Within a few weeks, I noticed a distinct absence of presence when we spoke. My intuition sensed he could be distracted because of another woman.

Acknowledging the signs, I chose not to worry about what he was doing or take the time to analyze anything. I was simply going to move on. I disregarded his ambivalence toward our relationship and allowed myself to become emotionally detached.

June arrived and it was time for my friend's wedding in New York. I flew up for the event and joined Driver for dinner for the first time since April.

It should have been an intimate evening, but instead it was the last dinner we shared. It could have been romantic if we were still a couple, but I knew otherwise and by the end of the weekend, he knew that I knew too.

I ended the relationship the following week, knowing it was best for both of us. I do not harbor any negative feelings toward him or how it ended, nor do I have any regrets. I enjoyed the majority of our relationship and the amazing experiences that came with it, and am thankful for it all. In the end, our parting was amicable.

What I despised was being belittled and made to feel insignificant and ridiculous. The comments wore on me, stripping away my self-confidence, one condescending remark at a time.

This, combined with being excluded from the most important part of his life, made me wonder if he ever saw me as anything more than decoration. Silencing me at dinners and speaking for me to project his desired image, emphasized whose world we were living in and effectively kept me under his control.

From this relationship, I realized the small subtleties can be the most dangerous. They are more difficult to recognize and comprehend, and even harder to defend yourself against.

I also learned that despite a man's elegant appearance, how he speaks to or about me in addition to how he treats me overall, are most important. This combination effortlessly reveals how he views me, and it must not be ignored.

Later that summer, a mutual friend of ours told me he was engaged. Although I was surprised because he met her a mere few months prior, I was pleased my intuition was correct and that I had listened to it.

This snippet graced me with an elevated peace of mind. It erased any possibility of regret and provided additional reassurance in my decision to walk away.

And in case you're wondering, I was not invited to the wedding.

Chapter 10

A Lil' Booty fer Yer Soul?

As I toss both of these men back into the treasure chest of life's various gems, I feel I must mention this next one. He was a brief encounter and played only a minor role in what I have learned along the way compared to the others. However, his approach is typical of many men who need to be called out for the sake of the unassuming female.

On that note, I introduce Money Man.

Transitioning back to living alone, I doubled up on my employment. In addition to the daytime temp work, I started waitressing at a bar during the evenings and weekends.

While working one evening, a customer seated at the bar asked me out. He was pleasant, handsome with dark features, and approachable. I agreed, and our first date was set for the end of the week.

We went to dinner and had a great time. Flowing into dating status, he immediately began showering me with gifts on a steady basis without the prerequisite of a holiday or specific occasion. I had never experienced such adoration and welcomed the positive attention for a change.

Thinking back to Driver, I remembered how deflated I felt when he gave me money (rather than an actual gift), for my first birthday with him. This new pirate was the opposite and went to work with grand enthusiasm.

Having excellent taste, he gave impressive, thoughtful gifts and they were always a surprise. In addition, he took me on shopping sprees where he encouraged me to choose whatever I wanted, and also moved quickly into planning trips for us.

One afternoon while we were preparing lunch, he mentioned our first getaway. He was setting the table while I fixed the salad.

"I want to take you on a vacation," he said, collecting the silverware. "What do you think about going to the islands for a few days?"

"Oh, that sounds amazing," I said, mentally packing my bikini and toothbrush while dicing a tomato.

"Do you need to ask for time off? Or can I make reservations for next week?"

"I'll have to tell the temp agency I won't be available. It shouldn't be too hard to get a few days off. When did you want to go?"

"We can go whenever you want. I haven't booked anything yet and want it to be fun and easy."

"Okay, let's do it!"

We discussed our schedules while we ate. As we talked, he realized that he could make one minor tweak to his schedule to free the desired dates. After that small change and before the dishes were put in the dishwasher, everything was in motion.

The following week, we were in a luxurious corner suite of a five-star hotel in the islands. It was beautifully decorated with earth tones and splashes of brightly colored accents that brought the local flair inside and denoted our arrival in the Caribbean.

We passed through the kitchen and tossed the bags onto the sofa, heading straight for the sliding glass doors. They were perfectly situated on the two adjoining walls facing the sea. We slid them open for an unobstructed view, allowing the salty breeze to edge out the cool, dry air inside.

Unable to resist, we moved onto the wrap-around balcony to embrace the sumptuous warmth of the early afternoon. Collapsing into the colorful hammock, we swung languidly under the huge bamboo ceiling fans, leisurely sipping the tasty tropical cocktails provided by the hotel.

The day floated by as we gazed at the pristine Caribbean Sea lulling in its endless state of tranquility. Succumbing to its soft whispers, we quietly discussed the day ahead.

"Let's go shopping," he said, breaking the sleepy silence. "I've heard they have the best prices on jewelry here."

"Okay, I'll be ready in a few minutes."

I finished my drink and went inside to change my clothes. I slipped into a lightweight, soft-pink sundress and pair of sandals. Humming along while braiding my hair, I didn't suspect anything out of the ordinary.

Ten minutes later, we were on our way. The day was sensually stimulating with the balmy breeze washing over our skin in the tropical heat. Walking hand in hand, we admired the colorful buildings dotting the street.

We were relaxed as we strolled along, enveloped by our surroundings and absorbed in the moment. Everything flowed and fit together perfectly for our first vacation.

"Let's stop in here," he said, holding the door open for me. "I want to look around and see what they have."

We stepped inside an upscale jewelry store and he went straight for the diamond rings. Rather than follow him, I chose to look at the elegant designs comprised of rich, deeply colored sapphires, rubies, and emeralds.

"Come here. I want you to try this one on," he said, waving me over.

"What have you found?"

"Here, take a look. This one is twelve carats. Let's see how it looks on your hand."

"Are you serious? That will swallow my hand. Look at the size of it!"

I laughed lightly as I moved in his direction. Having known him for only a month, the thought of wearing it left me unsettled.

"Yes, I am. Just try it and see. I really like this one for you," he said, reaching for my left hand. "Wow, I love it!"

His dark eyes were shining as he slid the crystal-clear, round solitaire onto my finger. The saleswoman behind the counter was clearly enjoying the scene, while I was inwardly cringing.

"Uh, no. That's too big," I said, removing the object and handing it back to her. "It looks like costume jewelry on my hand."

She accepted the ring and searched the showcase for another solitaire, per his request. I turned to him and spoke softly, confident she had heard it all before.

"I love the idea of having a new ring and you're very generous, but I'm not ready for *that* kind of ring. Besides, I have small bone structure and that one is too big. Why don't we grab a bite and then relax on the beach? We can look at jewelry this evening."

There are, at best, few ways to tell someone you are not ready for that kind of commitment without bruising their ego or hurting their feelings. Either way, I was nestled neatly in a pickle and tried to wiggle out as gracefully as possible.

He appeared deflated as I took his hand and pulled him toward the door. We had to move on from this location if we were going to discuss it further. Once outside, he shook my hand loose from his and shoved both hands into his pockets.

Looking straight ahead, he ignored me, allowing the silent treatment to set in on our walk back to the hotel. I knew he was irritated, but refused to let his attitude ruin a perfectly sublime day. Instead, I chose to embrace the serenity of the beach in a private cabana, letting him sulk by himself.

That evening, I approached the topic again, trying it from a different angle. He was sitting on the sofa sipping his scotch and staring out at the sea, immersed in perpetual silence. I walked over to join him.

"Hey, I do appreciate that you want to buy me a ring," I said, sitting next to him. "I want to enjoy this vacation with you, but we've only known each other a month and trying on diamond rings is too much too soon. If you want to buy me something, let's look at other things."

"I really wanted to buy it for you, but you said you didn't like it."

"Really, Money Man, you have to admit it was too big on my hand. Don't you want to buy me something that I love, too?"

Smiling tenderly, I pulled my fingers slowly through his luscious, thick hair, right above the ear. Moving in for a soft kiss, I held his gaze as I quietly suggested we find a compromise to make us both happy.

Acquiescing to my plea, he wrapped his arms around me and pulled me onto his lap. His disposition improved dramatically and our passionate kisses led from the sofa to the bedroom, officially kicking off our vacation.

The next day, we went shopping with a better understanding of what would please us both. While browsing, we found the perfect ring.

Sitting in the showcase and basking in the bright light, was a brilliant sapphire flanked by exquisite baguette diamonds. It was gorgeous.

After settling on the ring, he relaxed and allowed us to enjoy our time together. During our stay, we exhausted ourselves between the beach, sun, shopping, and incredible dining experiences and were thoroughly worn out. At the end of the week, we packed our things and the vacation ended on a happy and peaceful note.

Returning to the mainland, the gifting continued. The frequency of gifts increased, and my intuition perked up, questioning the possibility of a hidden agenda lurking behind the ongoing generosity.

In general, the combination of an attractive man seeking a commitment while showering a woman with gifts, may make many women swoon and fall into his arms with abandon. However, this was unusual for me and I wondered what the gush was all about. I was convinced that something was amiss.

A few days after our return, he came over and brought in a new TV. He set it up in the living room and handed me the remote control. I asked him what it was for and he said I should have one, even though I had not mentioned wanting one.

The following weekend, he arrived with an oil painting and suggested hanging it in the living room. He proceeded with his thought by searching for the hammer and nails. Finding them, he secured it to the wall with a sense of accomplishment and then turned for my approval.

I loved the painting and appreciated the gesture. I thanked him for the gift and, at the time, accepted how he assumed the task and completed it without delay. After all, I appreciate when a man takes charge and gets the job done without having to be reminded countless times.

Another time, he surprised me with the delivery of twenty dozen long-stemmed roses, with each dozen beautifully arranged in its own vase. With every imaginable color of the rainbow present, my previously unassuming living room now resembled a blooming rose garden. The delightful scent was overwhelming and my senses seemed to embrace their treat.

Later that evening, he came over for dinner. He walked into the living room, stopped, put his hands on his hips, and looked around. He inhaled deeply as he nodded and smiled, appearing satisfied.

"You know, you should give me a key to your place," he said, admiring the magnificent display of colorful buds.

"Why?"

"Because. I gave you a TV and painting for your living room. I should have access to a home I help create. That's why."

His demand surprised me. I finished setting the table while I thought it over, carefully processing his logic. I felt like he was pushing me and rushing the relationship. His request made me uncomfortable, and I knew I had to honor that feeling.

"Well, I disagree. This is my place, and I pay the rent. I don't ask you for anything. What you've given to me, you've done on your own. That doesn't mean I need to give you access to come and go as you please. I don't have a key to your place, either."

"That's ridiculous, Kendyl. You don't need a key to my place because I'm always here. How am I supposed to come in and set up a surprise for you, like the TV or the roses, if I don't have a key?"

"I don't hand out keys to my apartment. If I want to give you one, it should be something I offer when I'm ready. Until then, please respect my decision," I said, slamming the pantry door as I walked by.

Although I made it clear how I felt, I remained frustrated that I was forced to defend my position. His assumption that he should have a key because he gave me things made me bristle. In truth, I was on the verge of asking him to leave for the night.

Apparently, he sensed the need to smooth things over. He came up behind me, took me in his arms, and snuggled in close to try to soften my mood. But I was too perturbed to let it go that quickly, and gently pushed him away to fix dinner.

The silence set in as I went to work.

Chapter 11

Final Pass

Later that week, we were out to dinner at another amazing restaurant. We were enjoying the main course, when he told me about his upcoming business trip to Beverly Hills, California.

"I have to go for a few days in a couple of weeks and want you to go with me," he said, pouring more wine for both of us. "What do you think? Do you want to go?"

"Yes, I do," I said, buttering two hot rolls and placing one on his plate.

"You'll love it, but I have to attend a few dinner meetings. So, you'll have to pack more for that than for fun."

"Well, I don't have a lot of clothes for business events. I guess you'll have to take me shopping," I said with a wink as I took a sip of malbec, savoring the moment and the wine.

"That's a great idea. Let's go tomorrow, I'm free all day."

Already enjoying my salad, I nodded in agreement.

Tomorrow we would go shopping for something I could and would enjoy, and I was looking forward to it. Maybe we had found a middle ground on which we both could stand.

The following morning, we went for a leisurely breakfast and discussed the trip before venturing out for an elaborate shopping spree. We went to the most luxurious stores we could find and I twirled, danced, and strutted in everything we picked out. It was fun for both of us, and by the end of the day, I had a classy, elegant collection to add to my wardrobe.

I was excited about the clothes and the trip, and hoped he had moved past the issue of needing a key to my apartment. I wanted to be able to relax in the relationship without feeling pressure to give something before I was ready.

That weekend, however, he announced that he wanted to purchase a high-end, luxury convertible for me. Three days later, he showed up at my place in a black beauty he was taking for a test drive.

Gleaming in the bright sunlight, it was irresistible with the top down. The thought of driving it was exhilarating, and I could not hide my enthusiasm as I ran my fingers over the silky smooth hood of the car.

He grinned as he opened the door and I slid in behind the wheel. The stunning leather interior was exquisite and smelled amazing. Soft and sensuous, it was flawless. I felt myself melting into the seat and actually fantasized it was mine for a moment, silently taking it all in.

He leaned casually against the front of the car on the driver's side, crossing his arms and ankles. Still smiling that knowing smile, he watched me explore the would-be new toy.

"I'll need the title to your car," he said, breaking my trance.

"What for?" I asked, admiring the clever layout. I adjusted the mirrors and the seat without looking at him.

"I need it for the trade-in, obviously."

"Huh. Well…okay," I said, looking up at him over the top of the windshield. "So, you want to trade my car in for this one. That means my name will be the only one on the title. Correct?"

Springing into action, he jolted forward a few steps, stopping abruptly at the door. He thrust his hands onto his hips and looked down at me. His eyes narrowed, darkening to almost black and matching the tone his words carried.

"Of course not! Why would it be? It'll be in my name because I'll be the one paying for it!"

Slowly, I exited the vehicle and closed the door gently behind me. Leaning against the object of discussion, I studied him, taking in the entire scene. I was intrigued by his body language and instant mood change, and wondered why he thought he had a reason to be upset.

"I have to decline your proposal," I said, amused by the expression of disbelief that fluttered across his face. "You see, my car's paid for, and I'm not going to sacrifice it as a down payment on one for you."

"But...but it wouldn't be for me. Don't you understand what I'm offering? I want to buy it for *you*!"

"No," I said, turning my back to him and heading inside. "You want my car to be your down payment. If it was for me, the title would be going in my name. I can't afford to lose my car. Please, take it back."

He muttered something else, but all I really heard was the car door slam as I went inside. Obviously, he was angry at the rejection, but I was frustrated with his proposal and what it meant. Locking the door behind me, I leaned against it and realized he must have thought I was gullible.

The approval of such an arrangement would deprive me of any independence of which I would have willingly surrendered to him, making me his kept woman. I guess it was intended to be a subtler approach to achieve the same goal of locking me into a codependent relationship, after the request for the key to the apartment tanked.

But I was paying close attention. I was aware that if we parted ways, I would be the one struggling for transportation, while he drove off into the sunset in his shiny new convertible I helped him purchase. And of course, the top would be down with the wind blowing wildly through his amazing hair.

He was not easily silenced about the car and, like the incident with the diamond ring, he tried to convince me to want his gift. Despite his efforts to defend himself, I noticed how his gifts were objects used to gain control over me. Apparently, he thought I was naïve enough to blindly hand my life over to him.

However, even though I was frustrated about the key and the car, I chose to move forward with our plans for California. I was curious about what would happen when we were surrounded by his business associates and, in truth, I wanted to go because I had never been to Beverly Hills.

The day arrived and we headed out with my new wardrobe packed and ready to wear. The trip started with a bang, proving it was going to be a fabulous experience. We flew first class, drank champagne, and transferred to a limo upon arrival. Beverly Hills was as exhilarating as I had imagined and quickly stole me away.

Our hotel suite was as spacious and luxurious as the one we enjoyed in the islands. Equally stunning furniture and décor made for a welcome setting that took my breath away. After admiring the spectacular view from the balcony, I unpacked and took a hot bath in the enormous tub, which seemed miniature inside the massive bathroom.

Refreshed from my leisurely soak, it was time to prepare for the first evening's event. Wanting to make a smashing first impression, I selected the perfect ensemble and dressed in a pale-turquoise cashmere sweater and black silk pants.

I curled my hair and tied pieces back, allowing wisps to frame my face. The finishing touches included make-up in natural tones and a touch of mascara to emphasize my lashes. I felt elegant and ready for anything as I slipped into a pair of classic, black patent leather pumps.

We went to dinner and joined his associates at the large round table where he introduced me to everyone. I sat quietly, taking in the extravagant display of delicious dishes in front of me. I listened to the conversation, but as it pertained to business, it was difficult to participate.

After the main course, conversation turned to more casual topics and a couple of people tried to include me. They asked a few questions, nothing too personal, but definitely questions meant for me.

Immediately, Money Man put his arm tightly around my shoulders, pulling me close to his side and almost off my chair. He spoke for me, making it clear to everyone that I was not to speak.

I tried to free myself from his grasp to sit upright, while shooting him an inquisitive look. I refused to cause a scene in front of the others, but this was ridiculous. Embarrassed, I glanced around the table and saw the message was received. I was not to be spoken to.

I was meant to decorate and provide him with the necessary date to balance out the couples at the table. It felt peculiarly similar to the dinners with Driver and his clients, and I resented it.

Several minutes later, I excused myself from the table. Claiming jet lag to prevent a public discussion, I told Money Man I would meet him later, back at the room.

He stood to join me, informing everyone he didn't want me to be alone. We talked about the sumptuous meal on the elevator, and I apologized for being exhausted. As we entered our room, I suggested he rejoin his peers.

"It's been a long day," I said, tossing my handbag onto the sofa. I sat next to it, took my shoes off, and began rubbing my feet.

He loosened his tie and took his jacket off, placing it on the back of a chair. When he sat to remove his shoes, I realized he planned on staying in and knew I needed to be more persuasive.

"I'm not used to the time change and want to call it a night. Please go enjoy the evening with your friends."

"Why would I do that, when you're up here?" he asked, sitting back in the chair.

"Because I'm beat. I want to relax, maybe watch a chick flick, and sleep. That's it. But I promise to be fresh tomorrow."

"Okay, if you're sure you're alright. I'll be quiet when I return, so you get your beauty rest," he said, standing. Smiling sweetly, he kissed me on the cheek. Leaving his tie behind, he grabbed his dinner jacket from the chair, said goodnight, and left the room.

Alone at last, I crawled into bed, reached for the remote, and mindlessly flipped through the channels. I was distracted while I reviewed our entire relationship along with that evening's event. Frustrated and tired of the struggle, I knew what I would do if it happened again at the next dinner. My analysis complete, I settled on a movie, snuggled in, and fell asleep.

The next day, we went to an elegant, upscale restaurant for a late breakfast. The gorgeous, size-four hostess scanned him quickly while greeting us with a flash of her perfect smile. Her white teeth matched her fitted, low-cut, knee-length white dress and four-inch stilettos. I couldn't help but notice her medically enhanced breasts and thought she wore them well.

Confirming our reservation, she sashayed through the restaurant to the terrace, whisking us to our linen-covered table. After seating us in the sunken garden next to several celebrities, she turned and sashayed away.

The server promptly appeared, also sporting a perfect white smile and well-proportioned fake boobs. *Did everyone have them in this town?* She presented two mimosas in delicate, crystal champagne flutes before straightening her fitted, low-cut, white jacket and taking our order.

Our breakfast was divine. Emulating food designed for angels, it arrived on fine white china via three different servers who were all dressed in white with matching white gloves.

We indulged in eggs Benedict prepared to perfection, mouth-watering croissants still warm from the oven, and chilled fruit salads. While enjoying the meal, view, and ambiance, I thought about the upcoming evening's event and hoped it would be better than last night's experience.

Finishing breakfast, we moved on to window shopping and sightseeing before meeting his associates for another outstanding meal. Business was discussed for the first half and then as usual, conversation turned to lighter, more casual topics.

Once again, someone tried to include me and again, Money Man shut it down. This time, however, I chose to stay and play by his rules. When the evening came to a cordial close, we returned to our room.

I sank into the plush sofa and peeled off my stilettos. Rubbing my feet, I knew I had to address the issue. Even though I was tired, I knew it would fester and I wouldn't be able to sleep anyway. Sighing, I jumped in.

"Why do you treat me like a paid companion? I don't like it."

"What are you talking about?" he asked, his eyes glaring.

"You know exactly what I'm talking about," I said, standing and matching his glare. "Don't take me for an idiot, it's insulting. I'm *not* your object, but you treat me like one, especially in front of others. I've tried to figure out why, but it doesn't matter. It doesn't work for me, and you should know that by now. But, because you plead ignorance, here it is: we're done. I want to go home, and I want to go tonight. I refuse to stay and allow you to treat me like this."

"What?" he yelled, whipping his jacket at the chair. "You're breaking up with me? In *California*? How *dare* you humiliate me like this!"

"Oh, please!" I shouted back, grabbing my suitcase and tossing it on the bed. "You humiliated me in front of them *twice*! And you're accusing *me* of humiliating *you*? That's my point. You only want me around to make you look good. Apparently, I'm not even supposed to speak! You're too possessive. I can't be what you want."

"Really?" he asked, looking at me with disdain. "After everything I've given to you?"

"No!" I shouted, pitching my clothes into the case and throwing him a dirty look. "Don't turn this back on me! This is about how you treat me, and you know it. Don't make me sound ungrateful for your gifts that always come with strings attached!"

"You're going to talk to me like that? Then you do need to leave! You're out of here tonight," he said, yanking the phone from the nightstand and calling the airline.

When he hung up, he threw the flight details on the bed. Standing in the doorway, he put his hands on his hips and studied me with a heated gaze while I packed. After a few minutes, he shook his head, grabbed his wallet, and headed for the door. His hand was on the doorknob when he turned halfway toward me.

"I should've known you weren't worth the investment," he said, scanning me. He huffed and left, allowing the door to close behind him.

Unaffected by his comment, I finished packing and left the key on the dresser. Arriving curbside, the limo driver opened the door and I slid into the back seat for the last time, sighing with relief that it was over.

I had analyzed everything that made me uncomfortable and knew I was incapable of becoming what he wanted. His determination to make it happen was driving me crazy and I wanted out.

I decided that he thought he could purchase me and I was pleased to have seen the red flags when I did. Through material gifts, trips, and fancy talk, he thought he could buy my independence with the seemingly endless array of brilliantly shiny distractions.

Please do not misunderstand me. I loved the attention, new wardrobe, and exciting things he brought into my world. And, yes, I know there are plenty of people who provide a luxurious lifestyle for their mate without strings attached. However, even though our relationship appeared glamorous on the surface, it was a different story in reality.

One of the lessons I learned from this experience is the importance of recognizing true gifts and acts of service. Those reflecting genuine affection ask for nothing in return, while those given with the expectation of something in return (in my opinion), are not true gifts.

Instead, they appear to be given with an ulterior motive, such as with the intent of buying one's freedom and identity. That probably sounds extreme, but in this pirate's case, the booty he presented was definitely intended to be sufficient bounty for my soul.

After he returned to Florida, he realized I was serious about ending the relationship. Upon clarification, he made his final pass and threatened to sue me for the gifts he had given, claiming they were all a loan. It was in that moment my analysis pertaining to the convertible was confirmed, and I was relieved to have honored it.

I responded to his threat even though I had no intention of paying him for anything. I told him I would be happy to reimburse him for everything he could prove I agreed to pay him for, while sitting with legal counsel. Because we had neither discussed nor agreed upon him loaning me anything at any time, when he heard that, he disappeared.

And so, I bid you goodbye, Money Man.

I enjoyed the trip to the islands, love the clothes, the beautiful jewelry, and luxurious experiences. Thank you for all of them. I only wish your gifting was because you genuinely adored me, rather than because you wished to own me.

Therefore, I must request that you never resurface. Neither you, nor your gifting, are missed. And the supposed gold coin in the treasure chest representing our experiences is tarnished, revealing everything you promised was never even real.

Chapter 12

A Corsair Claims His Beauty

In case you have not taken the liberty to connect the dots, I will be forth-coming in confessing that during this time of my life, I moved directly from one pirate to the next. The men continued to present themselves, providing me with a full dance card, and oh, how I love to dance!

It felt natural for my relationships to be seamlessly woven together, without time or space between one ending and the next beginning. Because of this, I was unaware at the time that a change in my status would prove to be beneficial in many ways.

In addition and through reflection, I also discovered that how long a relationship lasts has little to do with the effect it can have on a person. It appears that how heavily we allow ourselves to become invested is what determines the depth of the cut when all is said and done.

That said, this next relationship, brief but powerful, spanned only five months. In total, it lasted a mere two months longer than the time spent being bedazzled by Money Man.

However, the impact was profound in what it taught me, similar to that of the amount of damage a tornado unleashes during its fleeting contact. Therefore, without further ado, allow me to shuffle through the glittering collection of coins and pull out this handsome devil.

It was a girls' night out and I was dancing freely on the bar, lost in my element. I felt someone's stare and glanced into the crowd. My eyes landed on a perfect male specimen staring at me with piercing, midnight-blue eyes, and I could not peel mine away.

I continued dancing while I evaluated his appearance. Quite simply, this 5'10", beautifully tanned Casanova, captured me at first sight.

He was striking with thick, velvety black hair, and an amazing smile. Although his steady gaze should have made me nervous, it didn't. Instead, I decided that if he was interested, he would have to make the first move. In the meantime, I continued swaying to the rhythm while I enjoyed the view.

As my eyes drank him in, I noticed the six-pack under his T-shirt when he took a sip of his beer. I knew he was trim, but this guy was in shape. He probably didn't have an ounce of body fat.

He appeared to be easy going, leaning to one side with his hand resting in the front pocket of his faded jeans. Brown leather flip-flops accentuated his casual demeanor; he looked like he had all the time in the world.

He waited out the song, standing still on the dance floor amongst all the moving bodies. The chaos swirled around him, becoming a blur as his stare intensified. I wasn't sure which was more attractive, his physical appearance or his unwavering presence. But it didn't matter, I was already intrigued.

After the song finished, I left the bar top and asked the bartender for a glass of water. When I turned around, I discovered he had put one foot in front of the other.

Having crossed the floor, he was now inches away, smiling a sexy grin while his alluring gaze burned through me. He introduced himself and asked if we could go outside to talk.

I told my friends where I was going and then we stepped out into the moonlit night. The nightclub was located on the Intracoastal, and the ideal place for us to perch was on the sea wall across the street. There, sitting under the stars on that warm, balmy night, we connected instantly with sparks of unstoppable chemistry flying and heated anticipation in the air.

Exchanging numbers before parting ways, we started dating without delay. We discovered how much we had in common, and our relationship immediately took off.

We quickly became a steady item and found we were equally content spending our time together with friends or on our own. We loved playing board games, rollerblading, swimming, biking, and cooking dinner together. It wasn't long before we were spending all of our time in each other's company.

Two months after that first delicious encounter, Casanova came up behind me while I was fixing dinner. He wrapped his arms around my waist and placed his chin on my shoulder.

"What do you think about living together?" he asked. "I know your lease isn't up yet, but rather than renew, move in with me instead. We can quit the thirty-minute commute and spend more time together."

"Wow, I hadn't thought of it," I said, turning to face him. "That's only two months away. Are you sure you want—"

"Shhh . . . yes," he said, kissing me softly. "I love you and want to be with you. I can get rid of my furniture to make room for yours, redecorate the place, and then it will be ours, not mine."

I considered his proposal as he tightened his arms around my waist. We were moving along fast, but with the pieces fitting together effortlessly, it felt like we were heading in the right direction. I realized his logic was hard to argue and had to admit, his suggestion was exciting.

Staring into my eyes, he waited patiently. When he knew I was coming around, he smiled his sensational smile and nodded several times like a salesman itching for a close.

"Okay, okay!" I said, laughing at his expression. "Yes, let's do it!"

He laughed, pulled me closer, and kissed me long and deep. When he drew back, his eyes were sparkling and warm with affection.

"I love you. I can't wait, it'll be awesome," he whispered. Taking my hand, he kissed it and then led me to the bedroom.

Dinner would have to wait.

Chapter 13

The Pirate Belays His Woman

The day arrived when my things became meshed with his, his home became mine, and it was officially ours. New to the area, I took a stress-free job for the summer cleaning swimming pools, while leisurely considering other options. I was at peace and enjoying life, oblivious to anything outside my little world. Everything was perfect.

For two weeks.

And then, as if I had been lost in a dream all along, everything changed. Go ahead, snap your fingers. It happened that fast, and just like that.

After the first two weeks of sharing our living space, Casanova came home from work one afternoon and chose to ignore me. He fixed dinner on the grill, but this time, only for himself.

He sat down at my dining room table and ate alone in silence. After finishing his dinner, he showered and left. He did this all without saying one word, despite my efforts to engage him in conversation.

This became his new nightly routine, varying only slightly between the days. He came home another time and flashed his beautiful smile while announcing that he was going to play tennis with his friends.

Those few words were the most he had spoken in days. And yet another time, he returned home to let me know he was going rollerblading with the guys and again, he left.

These were activities we enjoyed together. However, now he appeared to be absorbed in selfish delight as he flaunted doing everything with everyone else, while making it clear that I was not invited. It was as if he were silently taunting me, and I understood the message.

"See? My life is great. You've moved away from your friends and I can do whatever I want while you sit here alone, paying me rent. I have you right where I want you without compromising my bachelor lifestyle."

I was disheartened and confused. After a few days, I decided to address it with him while he fixed dinner, hoping to understand what was happening. I didn't know what else to do, but knew I had to try something.

"Casanova, what's going on? Why are you acting like I don't exist?"

He prepared the chicken and returned the sauce to the refrigerator in silence. He neither glanced in my direction, nor acknowledged having heard me.

"Casanova, look at me. Tell me what the problem is. I don't know how to fix this unless you talk to me."

He remained focused as he gathered his utensils and took them to the dining room table, setting a seating for one. He poured his drink and stirred the noodles on the stove. When his dinner was ready, he made his plate. As he headed for the table, I was standing in the doorway, blocking the entrance to the dining room.

He stopped, but looked over the top of my head, into the distance. Holding his plate and beverage, he waited patiently for me to move. He stood resolute and silent as a Greek statue, appearing cold, hard and lifeless, without a trace of emotion in his eyes.

After a long, painful moment, I turned and left, leaving him to dine alone. Crushed by his callous rejection, I retreated upstairs to the bedroom to change my clothes. I had to leave and go for a walk to try to clear my mind.

When I returned an hour later, my head was still in a complete fog and I was pleased to discover he was gone. His presence had become overwhelmingly forbidding, making it impossible to interpret how to act while in the same space. Therefore, I welcomed the opportunity to be alone where I could exist without having to cater to his unpredictable moods, embracing solitude more with each passing day.

His new behavioral pattern continued and, I must say, I was genuinely perplexed. I had given up my home, moved my belongings into his place, and changed jobs.

I was fully invested in this relationship and wanted to give it my best. I believed him when he said he loved me. I also trusted he meant it when he said he wanted me to move in with him.

But now I felt exposed and vulnerable, not to mention discouraged and pretty stupid. I contemplated my situation and realized I was in a tight spot, lacking the finances to leave.

I regretted moving in with him and was forced to consider my options. I had to find an answer as quickly as possible. If nothing else, I needed a better job and immediately contacted several temp agencies.

And then one afternoon, the silence was broken.

Casanova came home from work in an exceptional mood. He ran up the stairs to the bedroom where I was folding my laundry, and launched into conversation.

"Mark and Jessie are having a dinner event this Friday and they have invited us. Do you want to go? It'll be a lot of fun."

Shocked by the interaction and equally surprised by the question, I tried to collect my thoughts before responding. I was glad my expression was hidden before I turned to face him.

Oh, but he looked good, leaning casually in the doorway with his thumbs laced through his belt loops. His dark eyes were locked on me as he waited for my response.

However, I was caught between thoughts of how handsome he was standing there and the torture he'd put me through by pushing me away. Wrestling with wanting to kiss him and slap him at the same time, I quieted my mind long enough to give him an answer.

"Yes, I'd love to. Just tell me what time to be ready."

"Great! Dinner's at seven, so we'll leave at six thirty. I'm glad you're going with me."

"I'm looking forward to it," I said, smiling to mask my confusion.

Returning my smile, he looked pleased as he moved forward and kissed me on the cheek. He squeezed my shoulder gently and then bounced back down the stairs, humming happily as he went.

I continued with my chore, hoping the worst was over and we were back on track. He sounded happy, milling around in the kitchen getting pots and pans out to start dinner.

"Do you want grilled chicken or salmon for dinner tonight?" he asked.

"Salmon, please."

Surprised yet again, I was pleased he couldn't see me. Although I was uncomfortable pretending everything was fine, I accepted tonight's dinner invitation to avoid the risk of setting us back again.

Dinner was as it had always been. We discussed the upcoming event, and he chatted about work. It was strange. I listened in disbelief, wondering how we were having a conversation as though nothing bizarre had transpired between us.

We finished eating and he suggested playing one of our favorite board games, keeping schedule with how we used to spend our evenings. Afterward, we snuggled on the sofa and settled in to watch a movie.

We were spooning together and it felt odd to go from nothing to such intimacy at warp speed. He was holding me tight when his hands moved over my body. He nuzzled into my neck, kissing me slowly.

My head was swirling with mixed emotions as he made his desires known. I relented to his advances, hoping this was his way of making up with me. We spent the night entangled with each other and in the morning, he appeared to be renewed and refreshed.

Everything was back to normal. We had made it through the storm and fell back into our routine. That afternoon, we went to the pool and in the evening, we indulged in an intimate dinner together before turning in.

When Friday arrived, we dressed with anticipation of the fun social evening before us and headed out. Casanova put the top down and the warm night air enveloped us throughout the drive. It was perfect.

Even though we were greeted warmly by the hosts upon our arrival, I was uncomfortable when we made our entrance. Sensing hesitation, I caught the passing glances between couples revealing their uncertainty to receive me. After all, for all they knew, I was nowhere to be found during the past two weeks whenever they saw Casanova.

However, Casanova pretended nothing had happened. He put his arm around my waist and whisked me into the room, engaging easily in conversation with the other guests.

I did my best to also pretend everything was going smoothly and settled into mingling pleasantly with his friends. Casanova was warm and affectionate throughout the evening, and as we made our way around the room, I noticed the tension gradually dissipate.

Dinner was served and the lasagna was delicious. While everyone was seated, Mark mentioned needing a few volunteers for an upcoming charity event.

"What type of event?" I asked. "What do you need people to do?"

"You'll love this, Kendyl," he said, sitting back and speaking with easy charm. "It's an event to help disabled children. The guests will enjoy an hour with a speaker first, then dinner. The volunteers are needed to provide entertainment for the guests while they eat."

"What kind of entertainment?" inquired someone else.

"Funny, crazy stuff. Like singing songs, telling jokes, or embarrassing their friend; stuff like that. The guests will offer you money in exchange for doing something silly. The money then goes into the pot for the charity. We don't keep any of it."

"Oh, that sounds like fun," I said, turning to Casanova. "What do you think? Do you want to do it?"

"Yes, I'd love to," he said, smiling and kissing my cheek.

Several others around the table readily agreed to help out. Mark was pleased to have a group of supporters and provided the details for the event, which would be the following Friday evening at eight o'clock.

He told us we would have pizza behind the scenes and should arrive in costume. Casanova and I exchanged ideas of what to wear, while we all cleared the table. Everyone seemed happy and conversation was pleasant as the night came to a comfortable close.

On the way home, we reflected on the evening's camaraderie and agreed it was a hit. We were both looking forward to the charity night only a week away.

"What do you think about having a party on the fourth of July?" he asked, looking over at me while he drove.

"That's a great idea," I said, nodding as I placed my bare feet on the dash.

"Great, I'll call everyone tomorrow. After all, it's in two weeks."

He reached over and took my hand. Placing it on his thigh to rest and holding it there, he leaned over and kissed me on the cheek.

Once home, we went in and straight up to bed. It was a fun but long night, and we were exhausted. I fell asleep with happy thoughts of the evening. We were back on track and it felt good.

Things were quieter Saturday morning between us. He went deep-sea fishing in the afternoon with his friends, and I worked on projects at home. Sunday, we were both home together and to my dismay, he retreated into silence, once again excluding me from meals and activities.

Failing to communicate with him, I was forced to review events and conversations from the previous few days. We were getting along perfectly and I could not imagine what had set us back.

I replayed Friday night's event. I wondered if someone said something to him afterward about something I had said or done that embarrassed him. My mind was racing for a clue, but coming up blank. I honestly could not fathom why he was shutting me out again.

He continued as he had before, eating alone and making plans with anyone and everyone except for me. He made it a point to tell me what he was doing with his friends, always studying my expression as though anticipating a reaction.

Once again, I was thrown off balance. Silently, I wished he would go away and leave me in peace.

By Wednesday, he started coming around again. Thursday, he was more available, warm and somewhat affectionate, and by Friday afternoon, he was in full swing.

He was fun and playful while getting ready for the charity event. He carried on like an excited five-year-old boy, dressing like a professional baseball player and sizing himself up in the mirror.

Dodging him in the bathroom, I curled my hair into luscious curls that cascaded down my back. I donned a long, white sheath gown, wreath tiara, and gold arm bands, to emulate a Greek goddess. Instead of sandals, I opted for sexy, white stilettos with gold ties at the toes and around the ankles. Because my toes were revealed, I had a French pedicure to show them off. I was decked out from head to toe.

He came up behind me and put his hands on my waist. Studying me in the mirror, he brushed my hair aside and he kissed my neck. "You are stunning!" he said, still gazing at my reflection. "I love your costume, and I love *you*. I'm so happy you're going with me tonight."

Yes, we both looked amazing, but I was confused. I wanted to believe everything was back to normal, but he was unpredictable. Determined to have a great evening, I pushed my thoughts aside and geared up for a fun night.

"Thank you, me too," I said, trying to match his enthusiasm. Gently breaking free from his grasp, I moved toward the head of the stairs. "We have to go so we're not late. I have my change of clothes and shoes for after the party. Do I need to bring my purse or keys?"

"No," he said, grabbing our bags. "You won't need 'em. We're just going to Mark's afterward."

"Great, then I'm ready to go."

We took one last look around to make sure we had everything and then headed down the stairs. Locking up, we moved out into the peaceful June night. After placing the bags in the back seat, he opened my door and I slid in, relieved that things appeared to be back to normal.

He was animated with excitement and chatted enthusiastically while he drove. Upon our arrival, he grabbed the bags and then held my hand as we walked in together.

There was already a buzz in the air. Everyone was in a great mood but once again, I noticed the questioning looks passing between the couples. I had a fleeting thought that maybe they knew more than I did about

Casanova's recent behavior, but brushed it aside.

Although they were polite, they remained cool and kept their distance. Otherwise feeling confident, the awkwardness of his friends wore on my nerves. It felt as if I had made a mistake in coming, my gut telling me something was definitely amiss.

I took a few sips of the cheap, boxed wine and ate a slice of pizza before mingling. After a few minutes, I relaxed and began visiting each of the tables.

The event had come to life and everyone seemed to be enjoying themselves. There was a fun, lighthearted energy filling the room, making it easy to play along. I was having a great time doing harmless, silly things to entertain the guests, blissfully unaware of Casanova and his peers.

And then, as the evening was winding down and I had one more table to visit, it happened.

Chapter 14

The Proposition

It seemed innocent at the time, and because it was innocent and remained as such, well, it should have been perceived as such. But, it was not. Instead, it hastily became a tool.

"Miss, come over here, please!"

I turned to see if the speaker was addressing me.

"Yes, you! Come to our table next," an older gentleman said, waving me toward his group.

The entire table was laughing and seemed to have a trick up their sleeve. Assuming I was going to be asked to help them embarrass someone, I prepared myself for something that might be embarrassing for me, too.

"Good evening, how is everyone tonight?" I asked, making eye contact with each of the couples at the table. "What can I do for you?"

The older gentleman was grinning mischievously, waving a C-note in the air. His eyes were twinkling as he revealed his plan to me. "Well, I have $100.00 for the pot here, if you'll sit on my friend's lap," he said, clearly pleased with his proposal.

"Are you trying to get someone in trouble with his wife tonight?" I asked, tapping my high-heeled toe. With one hand on my hip, I wagged a finger at his co-conspirators and everyone erupted in simultaneous laughter. Tossing my curls back with a flip of my hand, I kept the mood going and asked, "Who's the lucky devil going to be?"

"This guy right here!" he said, grabbing his buddy's shoulder.

Several hands shot into the air, pointing at the target. The poor man was blushing beyond belief. I laughed and sashayed over to him, sat briefly on his lap, and stood to collect the fee.

That was it, nothing to it.

Yet apparently, it was everything all at the same time.

It was this one simple, harmless act that led to the immediate, public dismantling of my relationship.

Casanova instantly appeared from out of nowhere, wild with frenzy like a rabid beast. It was as though he was stalking me, lurking in a dark corner and waiting for the perfect moment to strike.

There, in the middle of the room and in front of everyone, he loudly accused me of being a slut and throwing myself at men. He sneered and shot off several nasty remarks I cannot recall, as the surprise attack made the moment an instant blur.

Stunned, I stood motionless in the middle of the swirling chaos. I was frozen by the shock of the ambush, trying to focus on what was happening while inside, my mind was spinning and my heart was breaking.

After his grotesque, snarling display of pure contempt toward me, I was promptly turned out by Casanova and his peers. He and his posse moved to the back room, gathered their belongings, and left without any further acknowledgment of my existence.

Before I could blink, they were gone and I had been left to tend to myself.

Wondering how things had taken a turn for the worst that night, I made my way to the restroom. Confused and distraught, I was clueless about what happened.

I had not acted inappropriately, been rude or embarrassing. I was not disrespectful to anyone, nor had I behaved like a slut (per his venomous accusation). Yet there I was, stranded without keys or money for a cab.

Methodically, I changed out of my costume and into the jeans and T-shirt I had packed. Replacing the heels with flip-flops, I was thankful to have them, given my new situation.

Placing the costume in the bag, I tossed it over my shoulder. It felt unusually heavy as I prepared to face the dark void of the night. Slowly, I pushed the door open, unaware of how much time had passed.

In a haze of timeless space through which I was barely functioning, I emerged from the restroom. I looked around and discovered everyone had dispersed into the night and gone their separate ways. Alone and bewildered, I started walking while tears raced down my cheeks.

I replayed the evening's events as I made my trek back those few lonely miles to his place. By the time I saw his townhouse, the tears had dried and I had a plan. Arriving sometime after midnight, I scanned the parking lot for his vehicle and confirmed his absence.

I checked the front door and, of course, it was locked. I was thinking about what I should do, when I remembered the upstairs bedroom window was always ajar.

Hoping I possessed innate monkey-climbing abilities, I began my ascent with the short, but well-placed, wooden trellis. Pushing the foliage aside, I held on to whatever I could and slowly worked my way up. When I reached the top of the trellis, I transitioned to any protrusion or indent that I could hold on to until I reached the second floor.

Through anger, hurt and determination, I made it up to the window. I heaved it open, pulled myself through, and fell wearily inside, dropping heavily onto the floor below.

Although the past few hours had sucked the life right out of me, I kept moving. During my walk, I resolved to be gone when he came home, and hastily began implementing my plan.

My first course of action was to find somewhere to go for the night. Immediately, I phoned a friend I knew would take me in at that crazy hour. When she answered, I apologized for the time of the call and asked if I could spend the night.

Upon her consent, I discarded the costume from the bag and replaced it with more applicable necessities. I grabbed my purse and keys and left his home in less than five minutes. I drove mindlessly to her place where she greeted me at the door, her brow furrowed with concern.

"Kendyl, what's going on?"

"Oh, Mandy, please let me tell you tomorrow. It's a long story, and I'm beat. I can't thank you enough for letting me crash here tonight, but truthfully, I don't have the energy right now."

"No problem. I totally get it," she said, dimming the lights. She went to the closet, pulled out a blanket and handed it to me. "Here, this will keep you warm. It's super soft and one of my faves. Make yourself at home and don't worry about a thing. We'll sort it out in the morning."

"Thank you, I'll see you then. Goodnight," I said, hugging her as I took the blanket.

With borrowed energy from deep within, I kicked off my sandals and made my way across the room. Tossing the plush pillows from the sofa to the floor, I fell onto it and surrounded myself with the warmth and comfort of her blanket.

Worn out and depleted, I passed out despite the torrent of thoughts possessing every minute, hoping when I woke it would have all been a mortifying dream.

Chapter 15

A New Reality

No such luck.

I awoke to the surroundings of her apartment with my new reality intact from the previous evening. She and I spent the morning commiserating over breakfast and coffee, the way that only girlfriends can do. I went over the details of the night before, and neither of us could comprehend how everything had gone awry.

After most of the day had passed, I decided I should at least return to the townhouse to see what might happen. It was late afternoon when I arrived and noticed nothing had changed since yesterday. He had not come home. What a rude surprise.

I was stunned. How reassuring it was, considering he knew I was locked out at midnight because of our conversation before the event. Still, he chose not to return. Leaving me, I guess, to sleep on the front stoop?

Oh, that's right. He left me at the event and leaving was leaving, no matter where it was from.

I needed to chew on this to try to comprehend at least some of it. It was extremely disturbing. In truth, it took a day or two for the gravity of the facts to sink in and register.

Meanwhile, Casanova returned to his home and appeared genuinely surprised to see me. Because I had paid rent and my things were there, I thought he should have anticipated my presence.

Why the surprise, my love?

The truth was grim and overwhelming and I had to come to terms with the facts quickly, despite being an emotional wreck. We were planning the party for the fourth of July, and it was already the first. How could I be expected to face those people again, let alone host a party for them?

Urgency became the tune to which I danced as I gathered my wits to form an escape plan. I went to work and tried to pretend all was well while pondering my options. By this time, I was working in an office and for the first time ever (and out of sheer desperation), I made a personal call.

As God or fate would have it, Mom answered the call rather than letting it go to voice mail. Distraught and in the middle of a breakdown, I barely managed a few words without bursting into tears.

"Mom, you need to fly me home," I said, resting my head in my hand.

"When?"

"I can be at the airport anytime on the third. I need to be out of here before the fourth," I said, catching my breath.

"When do you want to return?"

"I don't know. Can we do a one-way ticket, please?"

"Yes, of course. Where do I reach you with the details?"

"I'll call you tomorrow afternoon. Thank you, Mom, I love you," I said, holding back the tears.

"I love you too, honey. I'll take care of it right away and talk to you tomorrow."

I had never spoken to my mom that way before, basically telling her what to do without offering an explanation. However, she knew I was hurting and would do whatever she could to help.

It wasn't until after I hung up that I took a deep breath and started to relax. The reassurance provided by our conversation had a calming effect that allowed me to quietly continue my work.

I finished the day without falling apart, and then spent the evening killing time around town before heading back to the townhouse. I wanted to avoid being in the same space with him, but had to sleep somewhere.

To my relief, he was upstairs when I returned. To reduce the risk of seeing him, I opted to use the downstairs bathroom to get ready for bed.

Afterward, I gathered a few blankets from the closet and made a nest of comfort on my own sofa. Exhausted and mentally tapped, I crawled in and fell asleep.

The next morning was quiet while we prepared for the day. He didn't bother to ask about the previous evening, and I didn't offer unnecessary conversation.

At work, I broke my professional code again, and called Mom for the travel update. She had bought a flight for me on the third, God bless her. Thankfully, I could see a temporary light at the end of the tunnel.

That afternoon, I returned to the townhouse. When I saw Casanova during his private dinner hour for one, I decided to break the silence.

"I'm leaving town tomorrow," I said, passing through the kitchen.

"Why? Where are you going?" he asked, looking up from his dinner.

"Away."

"Um, well . . . okay. When will you be back?" he asked, swiveling in his seat to see me.

"I don't know."

I walked past him, straight toward the stairs. I was confused by his response because he seemed genuinely surprised with my news. I guess he thought I should be content being neglected and also excited to throw a party for his friends.

If so, then he could not have been more wrong.

I went up to the bedroom and finished packing as fast as I could. Ten minutes later, I headed back downstairs with my luggage, eager to leave. I walked past the dining room where he was seated and out the front door without saying another word.

I drove to Mandy's apartment and camped out for the night. The next day, she took me to the airport and sent me off with love and compassion. Leaving felt like the best decision I had made in quite some time, even though I knew it was only temporary.

It was a relief to go home where I could feel safe while trying to pull my head back above water to catch my breath. When I was at my parents' place, I found comfort in the strangest places and from the most unusual sources. I discovered the trip home was exactly what I needed to separate myself from Casanova.

The time and space created allowed me to start the process of sorting things out. I cannot clear my mind when someone is in my physical space emotionally and verbally chiseling away at me, even when barely audible through quiet, subtle innuendos and general neglect.

I had fallen in love with this pirate who had since ruthlessly stolen my soul without a care in the world. And now everything was different. I knew he did not feel the same toward me as he previously declared, and I wondered if he ever did.

This realization was tough to acknowledge, but necessary if I were to move forward. Adding the facts and examining the details, I shut down and became numb to my surroundings while absorbing the truth.

I know I resembled a robot during that particular visit. I might have appeared to be functioning fine from the outside, but if you looked into my eyes, I am convinced they were vacant. Emotionally paralyzed, I felt like a hollow shell of a being.

My family was supportive and understanding as they breathed some life back into me. Mom was a particular source of comfort and strength, as always. However, although she made me feel safe and protected, I knew I had to face my reality.

I realized the sooner I dealt with Casanova, the sooner the healing could begin. When I took charge of my life again, I would be able to free myself from the negative emotions rendering me helpless.

After a few heartfelt discussions with Mom, we agreed it was best to address the matter, before allowing it to fester. I decided to return to Florida after one week. The night before my flight, I chose to be polite and called Casanova to let him know.

"What time?" he asked. "I want to pick you up from the airport."

"No, that's okay. I arrive late and already have a ride."

"Kendyl, please let me pick you up. I really want to."

"Alright. I'll see you tomorrow then," I said, providing my flight details.

"Yes, I'll be there. Have a good night and a safe trip. I'll see you then."

I was surprised and, of course, bewildered by his response. He sounded genuinely concerned when he heard my voice and equally convincing when he said he wanted to pick me up from the airport. Although I found it hard to believe, I realized I held on to a bit of hope that our time apart was what he needed to sort through whatever had provoked him.

The next day, Mom took me to the airport and wished me the best of luck upon my return. On the plane, I sat quietly in my seat, avoiding conversation with everyone. I contemplated my situation and what I should do, versus what I wanted to do.

I was aware that in my emotional state, I was not the best person to make important decisions. I decided to say a basic prayer, knowing God would be more logical about this than I would be.

If I am supposed to be with him, please make him warm, tender and receptive. If not, please make him cold and indifferent. And please, make it obvious so I know what to do.

Well, let me tell you, some people may speak of unanswered prayers, but this one was anything but that.

Chapter 16

Heave Ho! Let This Pirate Go!

I arrived at the airport and saw Casanova standing there, smiling and cool. When he greeted me, he was not entirely cold, but relevant in warmth to a cup of coffee that has been sitting for fifteen minutes.

"Welcome back. By the way, I left the guys at the bar to pick you up. I'm going back after taking you home," he said, gesturing to the stamp on the back of his hand.

"Oh. Why didn't you tell me? I told you I had a ride."

"I know, but I said I'd be here. Let's just get you home so I don't keep them waiting," he said, grabbing my bag and heading for the exit.

It was a statement wherein an invitation was not extended for me to accompany him. His greeting was strange and I wondered why he had insisted on picking me up. Considering my experiences with him, I could only speculate the worst.

Was it to make sure he could control my return? Was he looking for a reaction? Was he enforcing his role by taking me to the townhouse and leaving me there stranded, knowing my car was someplace else?

The questions cluttered my mind, but I chose to remain agreeable because I was no longer interested in his motive. I was already in observation mode, hoping to analyze his actions accurately.

It was a quiet ride until he said he would be staying home instead of going back to the bar. I had no idea why he changed his mind and didn't care enough to ask.

Arriving at the townhouse, he switched gears. He carried my luggage in and held the door for me, dropping the bag in the entry. After I came through, he quietly ran his hand down my back, letting it rest low on my hip where it literally sent chills through to my core. I wasn't sure how to interpret his move and turned my head slightly toward him, my brow furrowed in inquiry.

"Don't look at me that way. Let me welcome you home," he whispered.

"No," I said, pulling away. "You need to tell me what's been going on. You can't manipulate me just because you want sex."

"Fine! Have it your way!"

He glared at me, breathing heavily with his fists clenched at his sides. Then, he turned abruptly and ran up the stairs to the bedroom, slamming the door behind him.

I didn't care. I was relieved to have the downstairs to myself and quietly prepared for bed. Taking the blankets from the closet, I arranged them on my sofa and collapsed into its safety zone once again. Trying to quiet my mind, I pretended to be asleep when I heard him coming.

He was halfway down the stairs when he stopped. I heard him lean over the rail as he shouted in my direction, "You'd better not be taking care of yourself under those blankets!"

I responded with silence while he hovered for a long, tense moment. Finally giving up, he snorted and stomped heavily back up the stairs and into the bedroom, slamming the door again.

Fed up with the mixed signals and completely turned off by his attitude, I rolled my eyes at his ridiculous accusation. *What a jerk!* I snuggled deeper into my blankets, comforted by the physical isolation the sofa provided.

Given nothing to rely on but my interpretation of his actions, I was left to assume his intention was to reinstate his control, manipulating me via intimacy. He required reassurance in knowing he still had me where he wanted me.

Sex *should* have made me feel safe and desirable. Simultaneously, it would allow him to regain his position of authority. The rejection on the table left him open to wondering where he stood.

That was Thursday evening. On Friday, his detachment continued as before, but I refused to remain in his home where he could access me. I decided it was time to be around someone happy and phoned Mandy. Together, we decided to go out for a night of racquetball and dancing.

I needed to pick up my car from her place, but most importantly, I knew we would have fun despite his attempts to smother me. I was also determined to cling to the slight improvement gained during my trip home. Refusing him the opportunity to permeate my space again, I knew it was essential to untangle myself from his silent, suffocating presence.

That evening, while I was gathering a few things to take to her place, he came in quietly and stretched out on the bed. He placed his arms behind his head, propping himself up to watch my every move. He studied me with his steady, penetrating gaze without saying a word. Within moments, an intense, strained silence engulfed us.

It was driving me crazy and I felt certain he knew it. I decided I'd had enough of his games and it was time for my definitive, undeniable answer.

Weakly noted, last night's attempt at sex could loosely be interpreted as his way of trying to smooth things over (although I think my original analysis was correct). I refused to waste any more of my precious time in limbo, waiting to see how things might develop. Even if it was clear to everyone else where we stood, I required absolute confirmation.

"Can I have a hug?" I asked.

"Why?" he asked without flinching, blinking or missing a beat. I don't think a hair even wiggled on his head.

"Thought it'd be nice," I said, shrugging indifferently and putting my shorts in the bag.

It was in that precise moment I received my answer, and I knew it.

He continued to linger for a bit, silently observing my demeanor. I proceeded to pack without revealing any emotion, grabbing socks and sneakers and tossing them casually in the bag.

He left the room with an air of distinct satisfaction with himself while I continued packing. I put a few more clothes in the bag along with my toothbrush and sunglasses. I left quietly a few minutes later, knowing I would not be returning that night.

I revisited the townhouse four days later. While I was gone, he didn't look for me and I did not check in. Upon my return, however, I was a different woman than the one he had last seen.

I was the person he met a few months ago. I had found my strength and was once again someone who knew who she was and what she wanted. I was no longer the confused, self-doubting woman he had whittled me into. I had a plan and he was no longer a part of it.

That specific day was incredibly productive. Decisions were made and acted upon that seemed to be only survival moves at the time, yet turned out to be life altering. Without delay, I started moving my entire life into a series of boxes, one piece at a time.

First, I rented a phone box for messages because, as you might safely assume, this was before every man, woman and child had their own cell phone. I was looking for a job and needed a number where people could at least leave messages. It would be challenging to communicate with me for a couple of weeks, but it was temporary, and this system would certainly suffice.

Second, I phoned the temp agencies and advised them of my new phone number from which I could only retrieve messages. I also told them I was willing to work anywhere north of Miami. In the past, they had requested that I expand my availability deeper south, but I refused, dreading the commute. At that moment in time, however, I was without direction or a place to call home. My life was open to brand-new possibilities.

Third, I contacted a massage school to inquire about the next session of classes. Before the call ended, the enrollment process was underway.

Fourth, I rented a mailbox at the post office and completed the steps to forward my mail. And lastly, I gathered several cardboard boxes and started packing and moving things into a storage unit, again in the shape of (you guessed it) a box! This, I must admit, is the squarest I have ever been.

Now that I was on a mission, it was important to maximize on my time. I was humming along with the packing process on the third day, pleased with my progress. I was thrilled to be taking action to improve my situation and felt empowered as I took control of my life again.

That afternoon, I was sitting on the living room floor going through the CDs, searching for my music. Thinking about future possibilities, I was lost in thought when Casanova came through the front door. He stopped in his tracks, standing silent and still, while I remained focused on my task.

"I'm going to play tennis," he said.

"Have fun," I said, without looking at him.

He remained motionless. After a couple of minutes, I looked up at him to be polite. Oddly, I saw the saddest man looking back at me.

Did you think I was confused before? Well, now I really was. I expected him to be happy. After all, I was leaving quietly. I was going without a fuss or fight and without asking for an explanation pertaining to what happened, how or why.

Instead, his expression was void of happiness or even the slightest hint of joy. In his eyes, I saw only overwhelming sadness. But I didn't care about his feelings or what he wanted. Those days were over.

As I continued my search, he studied me for several minutes in silence. Eventually, he sighed heavily and went upstairs to change his clothes.

But none of it mattered anymore because he was no longer a concern of mine. I was up against a deadline and had to keep moving.

My friends, Rachel and Glenn, were arriving later that afternoon with their truck and trailer to take the furniture to storage, along with any packed boxes. They would take everything except the dining room table, which had to wait a couple of days because of their schedule.

I was delighted with how quickly everything was coming together. Relief washed over and through me when I realized how soon I would be out of his home. Although I might not have liked what I had to do, I did acknowledge it had to be done, and was fortunate my friends could help.

The night before I moved out, his friend called. Even though we had met before, he seemed hesitant when I answered the phone.

"Hey, Kendyl...how's everything going?"

"Great, Brad. Casanova's not here, but I'll tell him you called."

"Um…thanks. But, what are you doing?"

"What do you mean? Right now? I'm packing," I said, placing more clothes in a box.

"Yeah, but, why are you leaving?"

"I'm giving him what he wants, Brad. He obviously doesn't want me here. He won't acknowledge me, so I'm leaving. Oh, and just in time for his birthday! Don't forget, it's the day after tomorrow, so be sure to wish him a happy one."

"Yeah, I know. But, you're wrong. He's crazy in love with you and doesn't know why you're leaving," he said, sighing heavily.

"Maybe he thinks he is, but he refuses to speak to me or include me in his life. If that's his idea of how to treat someone you love, then I don't want it. I have to go; I have a lot to do. Take care, Brad," I said, hanging up.

I didn't know what Casanova was telling him from his end of the ship, but it was irrelevant. I knew the truth and refused to pretend to be moved by his speech. I was living the real-life version of the relationship, and it was loveless.

I was sitting on the floor, mentally replaying our brief conversation. Unaffected by Brad's pleas, I realized I was proud to be moving forward while maintaining an emotional calm.

I was four days into packing, and the feat of moving out was nearly accomplished. Plus, I loved the idea of being gone before his birthday. Somehow, this detail made everything easier and a bit sweeter for me.

When I replayed Brad's words, I laughed out loud. An evil, witchy laugh, I'm sure.

My timing for the move, completed the day before his birthday, was poetic in many ways. Remember how he removed his furniture to accommodate mine? Well, now you know how he was greeted the morning of his special day.

He woke up alone and in an empty house, with only his bed and a few kitchen items. Refusing to be ruthless, I also left behind whatever I had given to him along with whatever he had given to me. I had a storage unit full of stuff and did not need any memories of him consuming rental or mental space. Let him enjoy them. It was over.

At the time, I didn't realize how the act of leaving him would later be collectively categorized as a major decision in my life. Following through with this set of decisions would take me places I never had any intention of going, leading exactly to where I needed to be.

In leaving him, I not only took charge of my life and moved forward personally, but I also reclaimed my sanity, peace, and stability.

I stole back the pieces of my soul that he had taken and crushed with the jarring motion of a teeter-totter, shifting between silent neglect and warm affection. I rediscovered my inner strength and rebuilt my confidence, restoring clarity to my thoughts once again.

I learned a lot from this pirate, even though I would have preferred not to have gone through the mess at all. In truth, I would have preferred to have been loved well and treated with respect.

However, since it did happen, then I am glad to have had this wretched experience for the lessons it brought with it. After all, I am choosing to look for the silver lining amidst the muck.

To Casanova, then, I say thank you!

Thank you for being cold. The emptiness you provided allowed me to take necessary action. Because of this, I was able to embrace the opportunity to leave you before I spent another minute wondering how to fix what I swear I didn't break in the first place, but could not prove.

Thank you for enabling me to create distance between us and become emotionally detached, like how you were toward me. It made leaving you easier.

And, thank you for teaching me how incredibly lonely it can be when in a relationship with someone who claims to love you, yet excludes you entirely from their life.

And Casanova, although I thank you for what you inadvertently taught me, I could never miss you after this. I do still love the handsome set of coffee mugs I left behind but, like you, I do not want it back.

Chapter 17

Weigh Anchor, Make Way!

I have learned to never underestimate the power or presence of true friends and family. I have been blessed with an abundance of wonderful people in my life, and am grateful for all of them. Throughout my lifetime, friends and family have provided understanding, stability, comfort, and at this particular time, a roof over my head.

Out of desperation, I left Casanova's place in less than a week and was not financially prepared to lease an apartment. Short on everything, I was allowed to drop anchor for a few weeks on Rachel and Glenn's sofa.

Their generosity served as a huge favor, and especially because they were married. A third person living with them could have been such an imposition, but they never hesitated. Their steadfast camaraderie assured me that although mine was a personal predicament, I didn't have to go through it alone.

In my new situation, I did not have a place to live, a relationship, or a job. I was not tied to anything. I was free to move and take a job wherever one presented itself, and an income was my top priority.

In unfamiliar territory once again, I needed to be flexible and willing to try new things. It was time to step out of my comfort zone and embrace change for the benefits it could bring.

The course I decided to follow was one I had repeatedly rejected. Finally surrendering, I moved forward allowing my ship to sail wherever the wind would take me.

Maintaining pace with the plan set in motion prior to leaving Casanova, I completed the enrollment process for the massage therapy program. Although it was not my first choice for a career, I had been told numerous times over several years that I had a natural talent and should pursue it. In dire need of any improvement, I gave in to the unanimous suggestion and changed direction.

In addition, within three days of agreeing to work farther south, I received a call for an interview. The company was located twenty minutes south and the position was for a project manager, starting as a temp with potential to go permanent.

The first interview was by telephone. After that call, I was scheduled for an interview the following week with the gentleman for whom I would be working.

Excited about my fresh start and eager to make the right impression, I realized it was time to go shopping. Although Money Man had loaded me up with new clothes, an interview suit was not part of the collection.

Determined to find the perfect suit, I went to my favorite upscale clothing store. It was my first stop because I loved their clothes and always found amazing pieces that fit beautifully. Plus, I didn't have time to shop around.

Apparently, it was meant to be because when I walked in, I went straight to it as though it had a spotlight shining on it. It was an exquisite black suit, tailored specifically for a woman. Classy and professional, I fell in love instantly and prayed it would fit, noticing it was in my size but the last one of its kind.

The fitted jacket sported a slim peak lapel and one-button closure an inch above the navel that would accentuate my waistline. It was cut short to grace the top of my hips and allow the fitted skirt to show off my curves through to its end, two inches above the knee.

Continuing to browse, I found an elegant, slate-gray silk blouse with delicate silver and pearl buttons that complemented the suit. Selecting one in my size, I moved to the back of the store.

In the dressing room, I watched myself move through an outward transformation with an inward effect. As I dressed, I quickly understood what was meant by dressing for success and how clothing can empower you. Gazing at my reflection, I felt tingly and invincible.

Naturally, I bought the ensemble without hesitation, high with excitement from my find.

Have you ever experienced a moment when you physically felt a surge of energy, or electrical wave, move over you?

Corny as it sounds (and I know that it does), that exact sensation swept over me when I left the store. While walking to the car with the irresistible black power suit in hand, I was literally stopped mid-step by the powerful rush.

The surge was surprisingly strong and undeniably real. The message was crystal clear: I was standing on the edge of my future.

I was definitely on the right path, and it felt long overdue.

I like to review this sequence of decisions because it provided significant life-altering results: first (and most importantly), leave Casanova; second, begin a career in massage therapy; and third, open work channels.

Do you see the common denominator between the three decisions I mentioned above?

I thought it was fascinating that I had to be removed from every one of my comfort zones to see the light. And even more enlightening, is that the decision to be uncomfortable before moving forward was left entirely in my hands.

Admittedly, I gleaned many lessons from this experience, but one in particular is noteworthy.

Because this was one of the most prominent learning periods in my adult life to date, I must note the crucial truth realized was entirely about me. Interestingly enough, it required the precise unfolding of events to reveal itself through the dismantling of a romantic relationship.

And here it is, the revelation revealed to me, about me: I had been resisting.

Absolutely everything.

Chapter 18

Shiver Me Timbers!

What a revelation! What had I been doing to myself? Why had I not seen this pattern before? Reviewing my epiphany, it all became clear.

I resisted leaving Casanova, maybe not for a long time, but trust me, I was fighting it. I was in love with the man he was prior to moving in together and wanted to be with that person. I was also resisting work assignments farther south because of the commute and hassle.

And, consistent with my willful nature, I had been resisting a career in massage therapy for several years. I feel compelled to expand on this last confession because over time, massage proved to be one of the best things to come into my life.

The truth is, I did not want to be a massage therapist. It's simple. While growing up, I had to give deep, exhausting massages to Dad to relieve his tired neck and shoulders.

The family would come in from a long day of work in the fields and on countless occasions, he requested I work out the kinks in his neck for him. The massages were seldom less than thirty minutes and often longer.

Regardless of the massage duty, my chores were still mine and had to be completed before homework could be started. And yes, after a day in the fields, I was also tired. Massaging him meant more work for me and eventually, it came to the point where I resented having to do it.

Later in my adult years, I often volunteered to massage co-workers' shoulders when I felt like it. But, then it was my choice.

When I submitted and opened the doors to this new career, amazing blessings and relationships began presenting themselves. I doubt anyone could have been more surprised than I was at the new experiences and opportunities that came from that one decision.

That aside, as I reflected on my revelation, I noticed an underlying theme consistent with each situation. The dominant thoughts dictating my decisions rotated around what I didn't want, which proved to be powerful.

When I focused on what I did not want, I brought it to the front of my mind. This allowed it to manifest, rather than dissipate.

I believe we should all know what we do and do not want in our life, lifestyle, and relationships. It is equally helpful to be resolute with what we will and will not tolerate from others.

This applies to us as well as other adults when personal, healthy boundaries and self-respect are at risk. However, once those parameters are defined, it's essential to move forward with conscious thinking about what we *do* want to manifest in our lives.

Dwelling on negative things or people wastes valuable energy and time. This habit proves to be draining and counterproductive, creating the environment for unnecessary challenges and obstacles to form.

The interesting twist on my confession is that everything I professed I did not want, wound up being exactly what I needed. In addition, what I needed held the key to achieving what I *did* want.

Once I realized this fact, I was able to accept that my goals and how I thought I would accomplish them, might be different in reality. They could even take me in unexpected, yet necessary, directions throughout my pursuit.

In summary, the culmination of these events produced the momentum required to propel me into situations I needed to be in, thereby forcing me to move forward in the direction I was supposed to be going.

This, ultimately, was the same direction I had been resisting.

Chapter 19

A New Direction

I was awarded the position I had applied for and am convinced it was because of my new suit. Within the first week of the new job, I found an apartment to reclaim my independence and relieve my friends of their houseguest of two weeks. I was officially moving on from Casanova.

Even though I no longer wanted him and was completely detached from him, the experience left me depleted. I was still healing from the harshness of how it all unraveled and knew I was not ready for a relationship. Therefore, taking the time to focus on school and work to rebuild my life, I refused all romantic situations.

One day at work, a new friend stopped by my office for a chat. She took a seat across from my desk, tossing her notebooks on the chair next to her. Leaning forward, she looked serious about her mission.

"How are you doing, Kendyl?"

"I'm great, Lacey, thanks for asking. How are you?"

"Good. But, what I mean is, well, how are you doing emotionally from your breakup?"

"Ah, that," I said, pushing my work aside. "Well, I think I'm doing fine. I hardly think about him anymore and certainly don't miss him."

"That's great. I'm happy you're moving on. Have you thought about what you want to say to him the next time you see him?" she asked, sitting back and crossing her legs.

"What do you mean? I don't have anything to say to him, and doubt

I'll see him again. He lives north and I never go up there anymore."

"No, you'll see him again, and need to know what you want to say to him. You need closure because you don't know what happened. Trust me. Figure it out so when the opportunity presents itself, you'll be ready."

"I don't know why I'd see him, but what if you're right? Thanks for the advice. I'll think about it."

"No problem, that's what girlfriends are for! I've got to get back to work. This was just bothering me, so I thought I'd say something before I went nuts," she said, standing and collecting her notebooks before heading for the door. She waved as she left my office, leaving me with a new line of thinking.

The following days were spent reflecting on the relationship and studying its demise from start to finish. Now that I was further removed, it was easy to review the course of events and how they unfolded, analyzing every detail.

I quickly understood how he played his part to perfection. He always acted innocent and harmless when others were present while undermining me the entire time. In front of his friends, he was as dreamy as ever, yet remained cold and distant when we were alone together. Unless, of course, he wanted something.

He reveled in his control over our relationship and social interactions as a couple. While contemplating this observation, I discovered when you trust someone, you seldom realize if and when they are manipulating situations to make themselves look good. If so, they can intentionally make you appear unstable and temperamental, while boosting themselves.

In fact, you may make excuses and start taking the blame for things like I did, to keep the peace and hold on to what you thought you had. You want to believe they were going through a phase and, on the good days, your faith is restored.

You want this. They comprehend it and, as experience has taught me, use this information against you. Playing off it, they allow you to dig a hole in which they will eventually bury you.

Consciously or subconsciously, this person slowly and subtly breaks you down, piece by piece, until one day you appear to implode upon yourself. This meltdown then serves as proof to everyone present that the theory the other person has instigated about you is true.

Their theory claims you are emotionally unstable, untrustworthy, or something else equally unfavorable. Because of this, you are blamed for single-handedly annihilating the relationship.

The incident now gives them the perfect opportunity to accuse you of destroying everything. The demise of the relationship is summed up as your fault and the meltdown has inadvertently justified their behavior toward you—past, present, and future.

Not only are you being held responsible for the failure of the relationship, but you are also held accountable for your new situation as though you purposefully designed it. A situation you might not have wanted, but are now in, such as being single after the breakup. As you can see, this could happen with any type of relationship, having countless outcomes.

In our story, the quiet neglect paired with his persistent gloating when excluding me from his life and social activities, set the stage for a reaction. Additionally, using intimacy to get what he wanted when he needed me for social appearances, naturally intensified my growing apprehension.

The culmination was the public incident at the charity dinner, used to supposedly give rise to our demise. Because I would not give him his reaction, he created one. And, even though he started the fire between us, I was the one the audience saw holding the match.

During my review, I understood that his outburst was his grand finale. Although his tantrum lacked a basis, I realized he caused the scene to create the illusion for others that I was indeed, untrustworthy.

The proof he staged was intended to validate any previous claims he made about problems we were having or why he chose to exclude me. The incident vindicated his behavior toward me and supported his decision to spend time with his friends, rather than his girlfriend.

This approach to creating problems when none exist is a typical ploy used to manipulate others. The result forces the unsuspecting person to experience unwarranted guilt, blame, and other self-destructive, doubting thoughts and confusing emotions.

The individual blindsided by this tactic usually wonders what they have done and how they can fix it. They apologize for the problem because they remain unaware that they were set up for failure. If successful, this strategy will undermine their self-esteem and lay the groundwork for an emotionally abusive relationship.

All of a sudden, I realized the review of our relationship was complete. The clarity of events from that night was amazing when the fog lifted and the cold, dark cloud was removed. Instantly, everything was crystal clear.

Thanks to Lacey's suggestion, I knew what I needed to say to Casanova to set my soul free. Now, I only had to wait for the opportunity to tell him, and then he would know that I knew.

Four months after I left Casanova, that opportunity came knocking on my door.

And I answered it.

Chapter 20

Thar He Is, the Scallywag

It was a girls' night out and we were dancing and having a great time. Although we hadn't been in several months, one of our favorite places to go was an old haunt of mine.

We had a blast every time we went, and this particular evening was no exception. The place was packed with happy partiers and we were on the bar dancing to every song the DJ played.

I was consumed by the rhythm of the song in an exhilarated state of bliss, when one of my friends leaned into me. She pointed to a guy in the middle of the crowd, staring at me and sporting a gorgeous smile. She asked if I knew who he was, and wouldn't you know it? I sure did.

There was Casanova, the scallywag, standing in the same spot he stood when our eyes met that first steamy, electrifying night. How appropriate, I thought, as he motioned to me.

Too distracted to wait until the song was over, I left the bar top and went over to him. He greeted me with unsurpassed enthusiasm, which was the exact opposite of the greeting I received upon my arrival at the airport months earlier.

I was surprised, and of course, confused, as I said hello to him. I didn't know why he was excited to see me, but refused to give it any thought. Instead, I pushed the confusion aside, determined to seize my golden opportunity.

"I've been coming here for four months hoping to see you! Will you take a walk with me outside?" he asked, literally tripping over himself.

I nodded my consent, biding my time to speak while registering what he said. Although it was loud inside, I knew I heard him correctly and had to wonder about it. After all, who did that? Who chased people out of their life and then frequented their favorite places hoping to see them again?

Keeping my thoughts to myself, I allowed him to continue. I was too busy processing the moment to interrupt, but also knew his excitement would enhance the sensation of the outcome of our chat.

"Come here," he said, guiding me by the elbow as we stepped outside away from the crowd. "Let me show you my new car! You look amazing! I'm so happy to see you. Oh, by the way, did you hear about Jessie and Mark? They got engaged! I've got so much to tell you. My friends can't wait to meet you, either!"

His chatter was hard to follow as I struggled to refrain from audibly choking on disbelief. While he was rambling on, I wondered why I should give a rip about Jessie and Mark. They were perfectly fine leaving me at the hall the night of the charity event along with the rest of his crowd. In fact, all of his friends were irrelevant to me.

Thrown by the twisted conversation, I felt similarly to how I did during the final weeks of our dying relationship. After several minutes of gossip and confessions about wanting to see me, I had heard enough. Shaking off the familiar fog I recognized from my previous experiences with him, I created my opportunity and took control of the conversation.

Smiling sweetly, I stopped and turned to face him. His eyes were sparkling with delight as he caught his breath and waited for my next move. The balmy night air muffled the sounds from the bar that always seemed to provide the backdrop for our most revealing conversations. It seemed fitting that what started here, should end here.

"I'm glad to see you too, Casanova. There's something I want to tell you," I said. I noticed he was eagerly anticipating my next words and it was refreshing to be the one controlling the situation. I felt I deserved his undivided attention and refused to rush through my moment.

He was fondling my elbow and there was a juicy air of expectation reflected in his irresistible smile. What a waste, I thought.

After a respectable length of time, I told him what I discovered when I reviewed our relationship. I revealed to him the one thing I needed for my closure and what he needed to know that I knew.

"It took me a while," I said, brushing his arm with my fingertips. "But, I finally realized it was *you* who sabotaged our relationship, not me, like you said at the dinner. I feel so much better knowing you're the one who set us up for failure and that it was never about something *I* did. I have to go. I'm here with people who want to spend time with me, and I'd rather be with them."

His face dropped, the smile vanished, and before he could respond, I did too. Pleased to have accomplished the mission, I went back into the bar to find my friends, feeling better than I had in months.

I did not hesitate or falter. I walked away without looking back and without regret. Lacey's advice was spot on and I couldn't wait to tell her.

The next time he would see me, I would be at a fair with a fiercely handsome, unbelievably sexy, romantic man who captured everyone's attention simply by being.

And yeah, for those of you wondering, I was back in my skinny jeans, feeling and looking like the girl I was when Casanova first met me, only better.

Eat your heart out Casanova. Your dessert is now on someone else's plate and it is *hot*!

Chapter 21

Cap'n O' Me Own Vessel

Work and school were going well and I was at peace again. In a few months' time, I would be finished with the massage classes and start working seven days a week.

Keeping the personal drama to a minimum, I refused anything more than a mild, fun flirtation with the boys. I was determined to meet my goals and didn't have time for a distraction.

After a little over two years, I had saved enough money to buy a house. Although this would not be my first home, it would be my new home in Florida and symbolized a brand-new era for me.

With the receipt of the mortgage and my new keys in hand, it was time for a long-overdue raise at the office. I asked my boss for not only the appropriate salary for the work I had been doing, but also the proper title. However, because I was familiar with the company's practice, I was prepared for denial with a backup plan in the works.

After my inquiry, I was instructed to provide documentation supporting my request. I completed the research and submitted a bulky report that detailed the statistics of Florida salaries for the type of work I performed during the past two years.

As anticipated, I was denied. I promptly printed my resignation and placed it on my boss's desk, providing a generous three-week notice.

I reasoned that if I were denied the increase yet stayed on, I would be silently agreeing my worth was where they valued it. But I knew better. I believed that by leaving after the rejection, I was creating the opportunity to live up to my self-worth by not settling.

If I am going to set a standard, then I need to find the strength and courage to live up to it. Otherwise, everyone will walk all over me and no one will respect me or my boundaries, not even myself.

When word spread that I was leaving, co-workers began stopping by my office to ask where I was going and what I would be doing. There were plenty of visitors popping in, because my position involved working with all departments.

Truth be told, and yes, you will probably find this irrational and as well thought out as my original move to Florida, I didn't know what I was going to do next. All I knew was I planned on working from home as an independent contractor. I wanted to set my own hours and eliminate the stress of having to go to a job.

One week after submitting my notice, a friend from another department stopped by to pay a visit. She leaned in through the doorway and asked if I had time for a quick chat.

"Hey Kelly, I sure do," I said, motioning toward the plush chairs across from my desk. "Come in and have a seat. What's up?"

"Thanks, well, I heard you're leaving the company. Is it true, or just another water-cooler rumor?" she asked, taking a seat.

"Nope, it's for real. I have two weeks left, and I'm out of here."

"Congratulations! I've kept it quiet, but I'm leaving too. I've started working from home for a company in Iowa. Do you have any plans yet? Do you know where you're going?" she asked, glancing at the door.

"Not really," I said, ignoring the phone when it rang. I reached in the drawer and offered her a mint. "It's just time to move on. I want to work from home and set my own hours. But enough about me; let's talk about you. I didn't know you were leaving, and you've already got a new gig. If congratulations are in order, they'd be more appropriately given to you!"

"Thanks, and that's why I wanted to talk to you. The company told me I could hire someone else to work from their home. You'd be recruiting for their project offices. The pay is great and you'd catch on fast. What do you think? Want a job?" she asked, smiling a knowing grin and nodding her head. "You know you do! There's nothing to even think about here, so just say yes!"

I laughed at her enthusiasm and the amazing timing of her proposal. She was right, it was a fantastic offer and before it could disappear, I snatched it up. With that, I instantly had a new job and before my current situation ended, my new position began.

The wheel turned and once again it was a girls' night out, only this time in Miami.

I was dancing with freedom and wild abandon, delightfully oblivious to the world around me. I was in one of my favorite elements, aware of only the pull of the music on my body and soul, responding to it as though caught in a trance.

And then the trance was broken when, from out of nowhere, he appeared.

Chapter 22

Blimey! Avast Ye!

Wow! That sums up the thoughts flitting through my mind when I saw this handsome, sexy man smiling at me on the dance floor. In front of me and close enough to touch, was a real-life romance novel's leading man.

Standing 6′2″ with the rock-hard, athletic build of a soccer player, he looked strong and confident, but not arrogant. His commanding presence put him in the spotlight, where he appeared comfortable.

I admired his attire, pleased that he knew how to dress for his perfect physique. The sleeves of his black, collarless, linen shirt were rolled up to mid-forearm and it was tucked in, accentuating his broad shoulders and trim waistline. I couldn't help but notice how well his faded jeans fit, with the sexy leather belt resting loosely on his hips.

Although he sought permission to join me, he was one of few I would not have turned away, even if he hadn't. Call me weak if you must, but I'm not sure any woman could resist a creature of such form and natural beauty.

We danced several songs together, moving naturally to the music. He was close and I felt his heat drawing me in, while he remained respectful of my space. A rare gesture indeed, his chivalrous behavior added to his appeal to make him more attractive, although that seemed impossible.

Entranced by his intense gaze, it was easy to see how he could make women weak with his pensive, dark eyes. I was trying not to fall, but knew I was losing ground as they worked their magic on me.

While silently breaking down my barriers, he took my hand and led me toward the balcony. We made our way through the lively crowd and stepped out into the steamy night to introduce ourselves.

He was struggling with his words, running his hand through his dark-brown hair while looking at the floor, when "Hi," came out in English. I picked up on his accent as he stumbled around with simple phrases and ventured a guess that he spoke French.

"Parlez-vous français?" I asked.

"Oui!" he exclaimed, his eyes lighting up with delight.

His smile widened and he seemed relieved to acknowledge he was French and therefore, had a great excuse for not being able to communicate clearly. Oh, but wouldn't I be the lucky girl? Thankfully, I took a few years of French in high school, and paid attention!

It had been years since I spoke the language and my French was broken and beat up at best. He didn't care. He was thrilled I knew enough to get us started.

When the night was over, we exchanged numbers and promised to see each other soon. I left the club twirling like a giddy schoolgirl kissed by her yearlong crush, convinced he was the man for me. And so it began with the sexiest pirate of them all, *Mon Homme* (French for my man).

Our first date later that week was at an Italian restaurant with an English/French dictionary on the table between us. Mon Homme was the first to reach for it to initiate a conversation, and he persisted throughout the evening.

It was a pleasant change, being with a man who wanted to talk to me. I was flattered and found it to be an appealing quality, even though it should be something to expect from a date.

The evening was fun yet challenging, as well as a bit nerve-racking. It was interesting, because we were both hoping to make a great impression, but could hardly communicate. However, the chemistry between us proved that night would be the first of many, regardless of any obstacles.

My French continued to improve, and as we spent time together, our status quickly merged into being a couple. He adored me, and everyone who saw us together could see we had the real thing.

As our relationship grew, I was surprised to discover how tender and affectionate he was toward me. It was a relief to learn he lacked the typical macho attitude that often accompanies incredibly handsome features. Thankfully, he had remained humble. Add the French, and I was hopelessly lost.

Being with him was effortless and felt natural as we spent our time doing simple, yet romantic things. We were easily entertained and enjoyed dancing, biking, walking on the beach, or going to the pool to relax.

One of my favorite memories with him is when he cradled me in his arms and walked around the shallow end of the pool. As he floated me gently across the water's surface, he sang softly in French. Peaceful, relaxing, and romantic, our days were filled with many wonderful experiences.

After Casanova (who was my last), this new relationship was a pleasant surprise. It was refreshing to be with someone who was crazy about me and genuinely enjoyed my company. Our relationship grew fast, and after six months, he admitted he was smitten.

I was home working on a project, when he arrived one evening after work. He came in and leaned against the wall, quietly watching me. When I glanced in his direction, I noticed he was smiling with a dreamy look in his eyes.

He understood my glance to be his cue and crossed the room, taking me into his arms. Holding me for a moment, he looked intently into my eyes before speaking.

"Je t'aime."

Framing my face in his hands, he gently pulled me to him and kissed me like I had never been kissed before. Slow and passionate, he spelled out the meaning of his proclamation of love within his kiss.

When he released me, his eyes met mine again, drawing me in. I could not deny it. I had also fallen in love with him.

"I love you, too," I said, in English.

The words sounded odd coming from my lips. It had been years since I said them to anyone and I was surprised I remembered how to do it, in any language.

After our intimate declaration, we moved to the kitchen and made dinner. Everything flowed easily and naturally between us. It was a peaceful, romantic evening and the perfect way to round out our day.

A few weeks later, I suggested he move in with me. He was living with his brother and sister-in-law in Hollywood and it was a long drive to put in twice every day. We wanted to spend as much time together as possible, and with him helping me remodel my place, I thought it made sense.

Aside from the convenience the arrangement would provide, the truth was that I hated to see him go and eagerly awaited his return. I was pleased when he accepted the invitation and moved in the following week. We quickly settled into living together and were steadily moving forward as a couple.

A couple of months later, I was still embracing how romantic he was with me. I know this is to be expected in a new relationship, however, after Casanova, I had lost sight of such things.

But, Mon Homme was different. He turned being romantic into a daily opportunity to prove I was always at the front of his mind. He knew how to make the little things linger throughout the day until I saw him again and he never missed a beat.

An example of one of my favorite gestures is simple. I was usually still asleep when he left for work in the morning. When I awoke, I found a freshly picked flower, often with a note. Sometimes he would leave it on the pillow next to me, other times in a delicate bud vase in the kitchen, next to the breakfast he set out.

In addition to being thoughtful and tender, he was also personable and tried to engage in conversation with everyone he met. My neighbors loved him and children were drawn to him, even though no one understood a word he said. He was a caring and thoughtful partner, sportsman, and dancer. He was the complete package.

"Well then, what went wrong?" you ask.

How dare I refer to him as a pirate?

Fair enough. Now that I have built him up, I must share with you how the relationship unraveled.

Chapter 23

Three Sheets to the Wind

Several months into our relationship, on a beautiful Saturday morning, I received a call from Mon Homme requesting a ride home. He was in Miami at the beach and his brother had left him. I didn't know why he was stranded, but it didn't matter in the moment. I was upset when I hung up and to make it worse, he was trashed.

My first thoughts revolved around his brother and I was angry at him for abandoning Mon Homme. He was the one who asked Mon Homme to go out the night before, and he was also the one who drove. There was no excuse for leaving him behind.

Muttering unpleasantries directed toward him, I found my keys and grabbed my purse. I locked the house and unlocked the car, hoping Mon Homme was in better shape than he sounded.

I started the car and shifted into reverse. It moved approximately three feet and stopped, refusing to move another inch unless I pushed it. The resulting inconvenience did not improve my mood, as I turned the car off and headed back inside. I knew the car needed to be towed in for repair and decided it could wait until Monday.

Focused on the mission at hand, I called my friend, Brooke, and asked if she could help. She agreed and arrived a few minutes later. I gave her directions to where he was waiting and we settled in for the drive.

By this time, I was madly in love with Mon Homme and remained oblivious to any writing on any walls. Or in the sand, I should say.

When Brooke and I arrived, we found his appearance amusing because he was covered in sand from head to toe. After a long night out with the guys and drinking too much, he had passed out on the beach.

Due to his restless evening, he was disheveled with his shirt now untucked and wrinkled. Squinting in the bright daylight, his eyes were slits, but I could see they were red. He was a mess and his mood wasn't fairing any better.

Although he thanked us for coming, he was irritable and bordering on being unfriendly. And, now that I was hungry, I was in danger of becoming irritable and unfriendly, too. Despite his mood, we needed to stay and eat for at least one of us to maintain a level of pleasantness.

"Are you in a hurry to get home?" I asked Brooke.

"Nope. What'd you have in mind?"

"Wanna grab lunch?"

"Yeah, let's find a place on the beach," she said.

I turned to face the groggy, sand-covered man beside me. He was rubbing his forehead, looking miserable. "Mon Homme, we want to eat. Can you handle it?"

"I want to go home, shower and sleep," he said, shooting me a look.

"I bet you do. But because you got drunk and Victor left you, we had to come to Miami. Now, we need to eat. And you should, too," I said, squeezing his arm gently.

I explained the context of our French conversation to Brooke. She was doing her best to remain polite while wrestling to stifle her laughter. Looking at her made it worse, and we both struggled to stay quiet. He truly was a sight.

We headed toward her SUV while discussing where to eat. He trailed behind, mumbling and stumbling along, sluggishly brushing the evidence from his hair and clothing.

We climbed into the front and Mon Homme slunk down in the back seat, pale and deflated. I felt his pain from where I sat, but could not pass up lunch. My sugar was dropping and I needed food. Brooke and I kept the conversation to a dull roar and after lunch, she dropped us off at my place.

This was my first exposure to someone who was so intoxicated that they were still completely inebriated the next day. And admittedly, it was not one of his shining moments.

However, because it was one reckless night, I blew it off. Had I known prior to rescuing him that he was that intoxicated, I would have allowed him time to think it through and sober up a bit.

But I did not.

I imagine because I rushed to bail him out, he took that as a strong indication of what he could expect in the future.

Now that he was living with me, however, I would gain more insight into episodes like this and the bearing they would have on our relationship. What I needed to learn would be taught via various experiences, providing crucial information.

This information would then be vital for making decisions where we, as a couple, were concerned.

And so the lessons began.

Chapter 24

Another Grog, Matey?

I know many people will see the Miami event as a red flag. And, maybe I should have seen it that way, too. But, before either of us are exposed to judgment that may be harsh and unnecessary, one must understand some of his indisputably fine qualities.

First, and most importantly, I loved him passionately because he was a true giver. He was genuine when he met people and they knew he was good, despite language barriers. He was honest with a strong work ethic, loved his family wholeheartedly, and gave his all to everything.

But he did have one weakness that could destroy him.

Mon Homme's weakness was alcohol. If he refrained from drinking, he was fine for a few days before becoming agitated. If he had anything to drink, then he fell apart. Sadly, he could not stop once he started.

It was scary to observe, but then, I am not a regular drinker and this was new to me. I admit to having overindulged at times, but they are few and far between and always leave me rattled the next day. In addition, I can go without a drink and if I have one, I have the discipline to stop before becoming intoxicated. He lacked this control and self-discipline.

The reality of his situation and the grip it had on him impacted his life in every way. I think the saddest part was that his brother, Victor, and his wife, encouraged him to drink. They found it entertaining that when he drank he would self-destruct.

It was disturbing to hear them mock him when they joked about it one night over dinner. Although I had yet to witness what they were referring to with Mon Homme, I knew it was anything but humorous. I had worked in numerous bars over the years and seen many instances of what happens when people drink.

Depending on the type of alcohol and its effect on the one drinking, it can alter and influence moods and dispositions, resulting in unpredictable behavior. As you may have noticed, people are affected differently, creating a variety of drunks. Some are happy, some slutty, others sleepy, and many even think they can sing and dance.

Mon Homme was the worst kind. He was an angry, mean, violent drunk who could not recall events that transpired while he was intoxicated. To me, that is scary. Imagine the horrible things you could do and say and the next day, have no idea you did it. That was what happened with him.

Only I remembered everything.

Time passed and it was another Saturday, when Victor called for a boys' night out.

"Vic wants to go out. Do you mind if I go with him tonight?" he asked.

"Of course not."

"Great. He'll pick me up," he said, squeezing my hand.

The day floated by as we worked harmoniously together on our projects. After dinner, he showered and dressed to go out.

Victor arrived on time. I answered the door and invited him in to wait for Mon Homme. Concerned about the love of my life, I brought up their last adventure together.

"Victor, please keep an eye on him tonight and, no matter what, don't leave him. Last time, you left him and I had to pick him up the next day."

"Yeah, well it's his fault. If he hadn't been trashed, maybe he wouldn't have strayed from the pack."

"That's not the point. When people go out together, they look out for each other. You never leave someone behind. You're supposed to help him when he screws up. That's what family and friends do," I said, keeping my tone in check.

Mon Homme appeared a moment later, ready to go and sporting a sexy grin. He was a real sex god about to disappoint many unsuspecting ladies. I felt sorry for them (okay, not *that* sorry), as my eyes wandered slowly over his beautiful form.

He was dressed casually in a soft, faded turquoise, button-down shirt and faded jeans. The shirt was open at the throat and left untucked, and the sleeves were rolled up to expose his well-defined forearms. Leather flip-flops completed the look and complemented his laid-back attitude. Simply stated, he embodied timeless sex appeal.

"You are too handsome tonight! I hate to let you go, but know that I must," I said, smiling and giving him a kiss. "Have fun. Remember that I love you and you are *mon homme*."

He grinned at the compliment, pulled me in close and whispered, "I will." He was still holding me as he kissed me again, long and slow. Taking his time, he seemed to have forgotten Victor was waiting to leave. "What are you doing tonight?" he asked quietly, playing with my hair and gazing into my eyes.

"I'm going to relax, watch a movie, and go to bed early," I said, lost in his embrace and inhaling his scent. He was warm and smelled too good to let go.

He caressed my cheek gently and kissed me softly. In the background, I heard Victor tap the wall impatiently as he teased Mon Homme about our gushy goodbye. We sighed as we parted and I walked him to the door.

He told me to enjoy my evening and waved goodbye as they drove away. Now that I was in a steady relationship, I had less time alone and was looking forward to my occasional night of solitude.

I turned in early and was sound asleep when he came home. It was around three in the morning when I was fully awakened by the sound of things breaking in the kitchen to the tune of Mon Homme's loud, angry cursing in French. I wanted to ignore and deny whatever was happening, but could not fall back to sleep with the insanity he was creating.

Reluctantly, I threw the covers back and sat up. I reached for my robe at the foot of the bed and pulled it on. Still heavy with sleep, I stood and slowly made my way from the bedroom toward the source of the upheaval.

I wandered into the living room, yawning and shaking my head as I shuffled toward the noise. I stopped at the entry to the kitchen, where I saw the refrigerator standing wide open. The bright light illuminated the darkness of the night, casting an eerie glow over the scene. I stood silent and still in the dark, squinting and watching in disbelief.

He was yelling violently while moving back and forth, methodically removing things from inside. Snatching the eggs and anything in glass containers first, he worked his way through the inventory of items in an organized manner.

It appeared his selections were in order of how fragile something was and by how many pieces into which it would shatter. After each item was plucked from the safety of the shelves, it was immediately hurled into the receiving wall at the opposite end of the kitchen.

The battered wall was now baring its studs in several places, with pieces of food and broken jars balancing on the edges of the holes created when something struck it. Where the previously pristine wall was still intact, the contents of the refrigerator clung to it, as if hanging on before tumbling to their final resting place.

Down below, the goop was collecting. There was already a layer half an inch deep covering the new floor of ivory porcelain tile, which had been meticulously placed the previous week.

Underneath the slop, a fresh gouge now existed from his tirade. Apparently, one of the jars landed at precisely the right angle to remove a piece of the tile, creating an ugly gash to be exposed after cleanup.

This mark would remain a scar to serve as a reminder of that wretched night, in case I dare try to forget the first time I witnessed his violence in action.

And the first night he threatened me.

Chapter 25

Tippin' the Black Spot

It was a long night. One full of violence and indescribable anger, and on my part, overwhelming sadness and total confusion. I will never forget it. It was unlike anything I had seen or been a part of before, and more like a scene found only in a movie.

It was surreal and relatively bizarre when I first saw him. He was physically present but consumed with rage. Out of control, he appeared to be an entirely different person. Whatever drove him into this blind fury had overtaken him and until that passed, he would be out of reach.

The night wore on tirelessly. Eventually, he realized he had depleted the refrigerator, having stripped it from top to bottom. It was empty.

I stared at the holes marking the wall while food remnants formed piles at its base. Juices, condiments, and egg yolk trickled freely down the freshly painted sage-green wall, blending together as they made their trek to the tile below. Pickles were scattered everywhere, mixed in with jellies and vegetables, adding specific texture to the colorful montage.

The gaping holes in the wall stared back at me, symbolizing the void my heart was beginning to feel. Everything was a mess.

I remained hidden in the dark, silently observing the madman in action while keeping my distance. I did not try to reason with or stop him, because it would have been futile. Instead, I retreated to the living room to wait until it was over, heartbroken and exhausted.

Apparently, he had no intention of allowing the storm to pass when he saw me. The refrigerator no longer holding his attention, he switched gears and directed his anger toward me.

I was surprised when I turned and realized I was his next target. I was shocked at the intensity of his fury. He was glaring at me with vivid disgust, spitting malicious accusations.

His words were mean and nasty, slicing brutally through the stillness of the night. He was infested with hate and determined to be as verbally destructive as possible. He was completely unrecognizable as he bellowed and flailed his arms. His rampage was in full swing.

"Where do you think you're going?" he shouted, following me to the living room with heavy footsteps. "Where were you tonight?"

Rather than respond and try to defend myself, I chose to remain silent. Feeling defeated and numb at the same time, I took a seat on the ottoman. I knew anything I said would make things worse and fuel his fire.

I also knew he was not interested in what I had to say. It was obvious he had made up his mind about the answers to his questions before asking them. He was on a mission and would not be stopped.

"Where did you go, and *who* were you with?" he yelled with clenched fists, now standing inches away. "You don't love me! You were with another man, weren't you? Tell me! Where were you? Are you cheating on me? You are, aren't you?"

He was hovering over me while my heart was shattering into a zillion tiny, worthless pieces. All I could do was watch as the man I loved erupted unremittingly with indescribable, unrelenting rage.

Although consumed with fury, he was surprisingly aware of my silence. I suppose to him that was as good as an admission of guilt to the charges he placed before me, causing his tirade to gain momentum.

Anger fed anger and the night painfully continued, with time moving forward in exceedingly slow motion. I sat still, frozen in place. Towering over me, he ensured my seated, static position would not change. He appeared to be equally motionless as his hateful, evil energy pervaded my space and filled the room.

I listened to him tear me apart, enduring his accusations in silence. He repeatedly rejected my feelings for him, calling me a liar and a fake. He worked assiduously to destroy our entire relationship within the course of those few treacherous, deep-morning hours.

My body was stationary, but my mind was racing. I wondered what had caused the intense revulsion fueling his eruption.

Prior to this episode, we were getting along perfectly without fights or disagreements of any kind. Everything had been blissful between us. I was at a loss; nothing made sense.

While my thoughts were swirling in a blur, a kind of hush took over the room. I snapped out of my daze enough to realize he must have grown tired of hearing himself rant. He seemed to have run out of steam and appeared to be close to passing out, when he summed it up for me.

Crouching down next to the ottoman, he rested his forearms on his thighs. He brought his eyes to my level, even though I was staring at the floor and refused to look at him. He sat quietly for a minute, biding his time.

Then, he leaned in close without touching me. Slowly, he brought one hand up and into the shape of a gun, making sure I could see it.

Placing the tip of his index finger next to the side of my head, he held it there for several endless, ruthless moments. He sat still, quietly waiting.

When I did not react or respond, he crept closer, his face now less than an inch from mine. He was breathing heavily and staring at me, awaiting a response. Temporarily paralyzed, I revealed nothing as my eyes remained trained on the carpet.

He sighed and finally broke the deafening silence, his words barely a whisper.

"If I had a gun, I would kill you right now."

Then, touching the tip of his finger to my left temple, he pulled the trigger.

Chapter 26

Tarnished Doubloons

Eventually, he passed out, face down on the living room floor.

Bewildered and stunned after his last statement, I made my way to the bedroom and went back to bed. I couldn't sleep, but with peace restored for the remaining predawn hours, I replayed the horrendous event in my mind.

I knew his outburst pertained to neither our relationship, nor me as a person. I also knew I had not said or done anything to set him off, and refused to take any blame for his tirade.

Nevertheless, I was perplexed and continued replaying the scene. I wondered how an incredibly wonderful person could become as equally evil. Two complete opposites resided within the same man, creating an anomaly I had not dealt with before.

At this point he is losing some of his glamour and looking more like tarnished doubloons rather than opulent gold, isn't he? Believe it or not, I was having the same thoughts. However, having fallen madly in love with him prior to this incident proved to be the one detail clouding any chance of reasoning.

I adored him when he was sober and was only now being introduced to this other version that was downright undesirable. Blindsided by what I witnessed, I needed to wrap my head around everything.

The experience that night was disturbing. It was even more unsettling when he did not recall the early morning's events, accusations, and threats, when I asked him about them later.

I believed him, too, because he was visibly surprised with what I revealed during the conversation. In addition, he looked genuinely horrified when I told him about his threat on my life.

I realized his drinking was dangerous because of what he was capable of doing. The inability to determine between right and wrong, combined with the rage he displayed, was terrifying.

That morning's conversation was intense. He told me he was not a good person and believed he was unworthy of a loving partner. The way he said it sounded genuine, rather than an excuse for his behavior or plea for pity. Somehow, somewhere, something or someone had convinced him of this, and I knew I could not shatter that belief.

I knew he did not choose to be violent, mean and nasty. Regardless, I could not excuse his actions or what he put me through.

I didn't believe him when he said he wanted to kill me. I knew he loved me too much to feel that way, but do I know that if he had a gun he wouldn't have used it? Truthfully, I do not.

After our discussion, he sobered up and became somber. He was processing the conversation and everything I told him. He even might have been wondering if I had exaggerated, when he went to the kitchen to make his usual breakfast of bacon and eggs.

However, any thoughts of embellishments must have evaporated like gas into thin air when he rounded the corner into the kitchen.

The holes marring the opposing wall greeted him, revealing its interior cavity. On the floor at his feet, he found his breakfast—swirled amongst shattered glass, empty containers, broken egg shells, and the rest of the contents of the refrigerator. Right where he left them a few hours ago, waiting for him to mop them up.

So much for breakfast, *mon amour*.

I hope you like your eggs scrambled.

Chapter 27

Seeking the Treasure Map

As you may have guessed, it did not end there. Should it have? Probably, yes. Rather than ending it abruptly, I chose to believe our love could hold up to the well-worn cliché that love conquers all.

This may be where you roll your eyes or possibly offer a heavy sigh of disgust or frustration, and I wouldn't blame you if you did. Or, you may relate directly to my predicament and recognize the emotional state I was in because you have also walked the same plank.

Regardless, I was in an impenetrable state of denial, and sound logic from which to make responsible decisions was nowhere to be found. Therefore, we continued on as before.

Under false pretenses, I must add. To the rest of the world, everything between us appeared to be fine.

This is what people do when they are in an abusive relationship, relentlessly seeking the treasure map. Whether they purposefully think it through and make a decision to do it or not, they often choose to believe the person they love can (and will) change. They insist their loved one is going through a phase and never meant any harm by what they have said or done.

The people who stay in such relationships are enablers who find ways to justify their partner's negative behavior.

I know.

I did it.

And not just with this guy, but throughout my entire life, starting as a child. This was something I had mastered, and it seemed like I had the message tattooed on my forehead for the longest time. I was a magnet, attracting anyone and everyone who needed someone to create excuses for their crappy, thoughtless behavior.

I was unaware that I enabled the problem to grow and persist. However, thanks to my experience with Mon Homme, I understand it now. I can see how destructive this tendency can be when dealing with any type of abuse, including that of an addict.

Time passed, and the fits of temper from Mon Homme became more frequent. To my surprise, they happened even when he went several days without a drink.

I am not trained in working with people who suffer from addictions, but if I had to guess, I would swear the sober eruptions were side effects of withdrawal. However, when I suggested rehab, he denied needing help. And then, shortly after that discussion, things changed.

We were at a friend's house, taking care of her pets one afternoon. After we finished the chores, we locked up to head home. While walking to his car, he became irate. I was shocked when, for no apparent reason, he started yelling.

The next thing I knew, he was inches away, breathing heavily and rapidly, as though out of breath. Hovering with his shoulders curled in, he glared at me with irrefutable hatred.

He was cursing loudly while pressuring me with his physical presence. Throwing his arms up in the air, he began waving his hands violently, acting like he was going to hit me.

Instantly, everything was chaotic and the situation became hostile. Amidst the confusion, I reacted without thought and slapped him. I was holding the keys when I hit him and the impact provided an intense sting.

He stopped screaming, blinked hard, and stepped back. I was shaking and horrified. It was the first time I slapped someone with force and it was a slow-motion, out-of-body experience for me.

I barely heard him apologize. He was trying to comfort me when he noticed blood on my leg from the contact. Through my fog, I glanced and saw it dripping from the cut on my hand, now trickling down my leg from where it landed.

Everything seemed surreal. This should not be happening. I don't hit people, nor do I create situations in which I need to protect myself.

My mind was reeling in a deafening whirlwind of alarm, and I could neither deny nor excuse what happened. Unable to fully process the details of the moment, I began walking home.

Mon Homme trailed along slowly in the car. When we were approximately halfway there, I decided to ease at least a portion of my misery and waved for him to pull over. I slid into the passenger seat next to him and slumped down, limp with mental and physical exhaustion.

I had been worn down like a piece of glass on the beach that the ocean worked over until it was round and smooth, losing all sharpness to become defenseless against the elements. I saw my own blood from a scenario in which I participated that would undoubtedly qualify as domestic violence, and it was foreign to me.

I did not recognize the person I became when I fought back. The entire episode represented the opposite of my personality, my expectations of a healthy relationship, and the kind of man with whom I wanted to share my life. I didn't know who I was at that moment and did not like it.

This time, I could not dredge up an excuse to justify what had just happened. I received the message loud and clear, even though I felt faint and lightheaded.

It was this turbulent event that forced me to step away from denial and admit the truth. In doing so, I acknowledged that our love could not conquer the demons reigning over him, standing between us.

Talk about feeling defeated and deflated. I was not ready to give up, but I was caught in the clutches of a suffocating grip and felt like I was sinking into a deep, hopeless abyss.

As time would reveal however, I would find my strength. Eventually, I would discover the love I have for myself would allow me to do one of the hardest things I have ever had to do.

Chapter 28

Me Letter O' Marque

The ride home was quiet. When we arrived, I cleaned the cut and took a hot bath to relax and reflect on the afternoon. He needed to acknowledge his addiction, and I needed to ensure my safety by addressing it with him directly.

While we were fixing dinner that evening, I was wondering how to express myself in French and remain effective. He must have had similar thoughts, because he brought the topic up when we sat down.

Looking intently at me, he took my hand in his and examined the cut. "I hate that I started a fight and you got hurt, so I'm going to rehab. I can't keep doing this to you, but I don't know how to stop," he said, the sadness in his eyes deepening.

"Thank you. I don't know, either. I think rehab is your best option, because I can't live like this."

"I know. I love you and never want to hurt you. Will you wait for me?"

"Of course," I said, tears springing to my eyes. "I love you. Just because you have something to fight, doesn't change that," I said, wiping the tears away. "When are you going?"

"I'll call my parents tonight and leave as soon as possible," he said, gently kissing my wound.

The rest of the evening was quiet, with both of us lost in our own thoughts. I saw the hurt in his eyes when he realized the depth of the situation and, because it was his idea to go, a tiny glimmer of hope was restored, giving me something to cling to.

A few days later, I drove him to the airport. We said our tearful good-byes and I was a wreck.

I missed him terribly, despite his vicious outbreaks. As is generally the case when you are separated from the one you love, I focused on the positives in the relationship and held on to what I knew we could have *if only* he could conquer his addiction.

We spoke several times after he arrived back in his hometown. The last time we talked, he said we could not communicate with each other after he went to rehab. It would only be for a month, and I was hopeful of a sober, loving man returning to me. I knew it was for the best.

The month passed slowly, seeming to take longer than usual. When it was over, he returned to Florida and it was wonderful to be with him again. I was thrilled and only somewhat curious about how things would come to pass, now that he was back in the land of relentless temptation.

A few weeks after his return, Victor called for a night out and Mon Homme could not resist. He might have spent time in rehab where he didn't drink, but he did not learn how to overcome the need or desire to drink. He was hooked again with one night of fun, throwing him back to the wicked position of square one in less than a heartbeat.

I imagine this is something the experts expect. After all, he drank habitually for over twelve years prior to going to rehab. I believe that over time, it became a physiological need and would require more to heal his body than the thirty-day stay provided.

If nothing else, it was definitely his crutch, the one thing he relied on to provide his escape when he was depressed or angry. It was also something he did when hanging out with friends to have fun. He could not catch a break.

He was an alcoholic.

Even if this was his reality all along and he knew it, I was just beginning to comprehend its depth and overall severity.

His addiction had a huge impact on my perception of the relationship and my hopes for having a stable life with him. Now that I understood his was not a case of someone who could not control himself when he drank, but rather that of an alcoholic, it gave me a different perspective from which to view things.

His relapse required another visit to rehab within a month after his return. During his previous visit, I seized the opportunity to gather my thoughts and made a decision that was not negotiable. I realized I had the choice to accept or refuse the opportunity to live in his world, and I chose to refuse it.

I had taken the month to examine my stance and create my supporting argument. My thoughts were and are simple, whether they be directed at Mon Homme then, or anyone else who brings their issues to my door.

You have demons? They are yours. Deal with them. Take charge of your life and don't let them own you. Do not fool yourself, pretending they don't have control over you, because they do.

Take a look around. A good, hard look. Be honest with yourself about what is happening in your life. Do not pretend the drugs, alcohol, porn, or gambling are not destroying your relationships, because they are.

Be determined to beat whatever it is. Find your inner strength. Ask God for help. Hire a professional to counsel you through the adjustment phase, which will be challenging regardless of how strong you think you are.

However you choose to do it, take responsibility and start. Get help where you need it and do yourself a favor: stop being the victim.

Find a way to prove to yourself that you are good and learn to love yourself. You have to do this on your own, because no one can do it for you. *You* must believe you are worth fighting for and find a way to save yourself.

You have to do this for you, and you have to want to.

As for me?

I will not allow you to pull me down on your spiral of depression and self-destruction. I have received my Letter of Marque and am stealing back that which was originally mine but was stolen from me.

I am taking back the person I want to be and the reality in which I wish

122

to live. I am reclaiming my self-respect and my identity.

I am stealing back my soul.

As far as Mon Homme and I were concerned, I knew it was time to take action and restore my life. I told him he needed to return to rehab and this time, for us, it was goodbye.

When we parted ways the second time, I told him he could never look for me again and although it broke my heart, I would not be waiting for him. If he truly loved me, he would let me go.

I made a commitment to myself that I needed to uphold. I refused to perpetuate the heartbreak by repeatedly saying goodbye to the man I loved, while sending him off to fight his demons.

Thirty days in rehab was not going to be enough to conquer what he was up against, and this time I knew better than to hold on to any false hopes. It was time to start healing from the heart-wrenching experience of having found a man who loved me completely, but with whom I could not build a life.

It was also time for him to face his problems and start fighting them for himself, without me there to soften the blow. It was necessary for us to go our separate ways, and one of us had to be strong enough to admit it and initiate the break.

Does that sound heartless?

I know some will see it that way. I prefer to think of it as tough love for him and self-preservation for me.

Every time he tore us apart, I was the one left holding the pieces, trying to put them back together to make us whole. I stood by him and proved my love, and yet it was clear there was no reprieve in sight.

Now, it was time to prove my love for myself, to myself. Enough was enough.

Mon Homme and I spoke a few times on the phone after he left, trying to maintain a friendship. When he started dating someone from rehab, it hurt to hear about her. It was upsetting that someone else might be a better fit for him, and if so, quite possibly because she was also an addict. Even though we were no longer together, I had not stopped loving him.

After three months, I asked him to stop calling and explained that it was too hard. It was painful to be reminded of what we had, always reliving the best parts of our relationship, only to be forced back into reality where we could not be together. The constant communication also prevented me from being able to heal.

He quietly agreed to respect my request.

Several months later, at two thirty in the morning, the phone rang and it was Mon Homme. He had been out for the night; the bars were closed, and he was trashed. He was slurring his words and professing his undying love for me.

I lay in bed with tears racing down my cheeks. He had not conquered his demons.

If I doubted my actions months earlier, then this phone call cleared the plate. I had indeed made the right decision when I told him to go and not return.

That was the last time we spoke.

Maybe it was closure I needed. Maybe it was a call he needed to make. I don't know and it doesn't matter.

I can tell you that, although he did not fully become the captain of my heart, he did hold a piece of it along with the unique position of having been a true love.

And Mon Homme, I hope you know.

Chapter 29

Escapin' the Hempen Halter

Mon Homme proved to be an effective teacher in how someone's actions can impact another's world, and specifically, mine. I realize many people involved with an addict might not comprehend what is happening to them because of the other's addiction.

I understand, because I was one of those people.

In an attempt to shed some light on a dark topic, following is a powerful set of lessons I took from my relationship with Mon Homme. I share these because they can be applied by anyone, and may even prove useful in assisting some to move forward from an equally turbulent situation.

First, I learned despite how much someone loves someone else, if they have an addiction, it will almost always win. Without professional help (and possibly a lot of it), it would be rare for the addiction to lose.

The addict will usually turn to a destructive behavior, often geared toward others. This might consist of creating guilt in their partner or loved ones via verbal accusations, physical abuse, lying, cheating or stealing to acquire what they need. Their own lives and relationships fall to the side, as the cost to themselves (or those whom they hurt), is irrelevant to feeding their need.

Second, I learned addictions are extremely powerful. Unless you are trained in working with them, you would be wise to let the professionals fight the battle. Please do not assume you will be able to save your loved one from their destructive path.

This observation is based on my experience, and no offense is meant to anyone who reads it. For me, it served as a reality check.

Addiction has revealed its power to me when it consumes someone. The person overtaken can easily become unidentifiable, unapproachable, and irrational. Trust me when I tell you, it has the capability of becoming bigger and stronger than what the average person can successfully and safely influence.

In addition, if you think you are capable of helping them on your own, you will probably wind up sinking with them. Maybe you will refrain from becoming an addict, but you are sure to be investing your energy, love, time, and money into a cause in which you strongly believe and they, more often than not, cannot relate to.

In the end, you will be living this truth. Maybe you'll be broke, worn-out, emotionally distraught, and exhausted. You'll probably look ten years older than you are, too.

The addict, however, will move on. They will continue searching for what they need, usually oblivious to the pain and loss you are experiencing.

Third, I discovered it is not my responsibility to continue supporting someone through their dependencies.

You might disagree with me, but I know many people refuse to help themselves. When this is the case, it remains pointless to try to force them to want change. Regardless of whether or not it could lead to a better situation, they must make their own decisions and I have learned to accept this.

And fourth, I know I do not have to tolerate and accept an abusive relationship of any kind.

Period.

I realized being in the relationship was a decision I made and one I could reverse at any time. I also saw us moving in opposite directions and refused to give up on my dreams and healthy outlook on life to follow him on his road to self-destruction.

After acknowledging all of this, I recognized that I owned the power to end my suffering. I knew it was entirely up to me to make the first move and stand by my decision. Although I knew how much it would hurt, I also knew the pain would pass with time.

In essence, I gave myself permission (and therefore the courage), to be brave enough to escape the hempen halter and walk away from the man I loved. I had to do this because everything revolving around his decisions and chosen lifestyle was destroying me.

To Mon Homme, then, I say thank you!

Thank you for loving me completely. You were the first man to show me what it looked like, and I will always be grateful.

Thank you for teaching me the invaluable lesson of creating boundaries to protect myself—and then for letting me go.

And on a final note, I hope you have conquered your demons and found the peace and happiness I know you deserve.

Chapter 30

Another Gentleman O' Fortune

I discovered an interesting detail about a relationship in which you genuinely fall in love. The depth and reality of your emotions complicates moving forward after the relationship ends, regardless of why it ended.

I think in this case it was more challenging because as a sober couple, we were amazing together and truly loved each other. So, merely by chance (and most definitely not intended), there was a rebound man.

I still shake my head as I pull this particular pirate from my treasure chest. But, being knee-deep in my story, I will continue.

During the remodeling process of my home, I decided to install granite countertops in the kitchen. While researching my options, I stopped by a granite shop on the outskirts of Fort Lauderdale.

The manager was attentive and walked me through the process of what to expect after selecting my slabs. I thanked him for his time, but wound up purchasing elsewhere. Therefore, I was surprised when he called a few weeks after our first encounter.

"Kendyl?"

"Yes, how are you?" I said, recognizing his number from caller ID.

"Great. Hey, I was wonderin', d'ya wanna be a sales rep for me?"

"Wow, thanks. You do know that I don't know anything about granite, right?" I asked.

"I can teach ya what ya need ta know. So, whattaya think?"

"Okay, if I can work from home. I'll still have my contract work and also the spa on the weekends."

"Yeah, s'long as ya make the customers happy."

"That'll be the easy part. When do you want me to start?"

"Soon as possible," he said.

The next week, I began my new career. I spent time in the office to learn the basics and quickly discovered I would be learning the business alone. I thought it was odd that he wanted me to represent the company, yet when asked, he was conveniently unavailable to provide guidance.

When I asked about the owner, I learned that his brother, Jake, owned this and another store. Apparently, he stayed at the one on the west side of the state and was out of the picture. Therefore, he was not of any help.

Fortunately, I was able to grasp enough on my own and after a few days, I started calling on clients.

I was busy learning the ropes and pursuing contracts, when I noticed his personal attention. He was overly friendly for a boss, and after a few weeks, he confirmed my suspicion.

"D'ya wanna go ta dinner tonight?" he asked one afternoon.

"You know I'm in a relationship," I said, gathering samples of granite slabs and setting them in a box.

"Yeah, but we can talk 'bout any questions ya got."

"Thanks, but I have too much to learn to go over in one evening," I replied amicably.

"Whenever ya got questions, just ask."

He smiled as he picked up the box of samples like they were cotton balls. Although he was 5'10", he was bulky and looked like he used to work out too much. He was still in decent shape, but his size and condition were probably the result of overdeveloped muscle that he had let go.

He walked me to my car and I popped the trunk for him to put the box inside. While he loaded it, I opened the door to let the heat out. It was another oppressively hot day in sunny South Florida.

"Thanks, I'll see you soon," I said, sliding in behind the wheel. I settled into the driver's seat, started the engine, and cranked up the air conditioning. I thought about his invitation on the way home and wondered why he thought I would accept, knowing I was in a relationship.

He was pleasant but not my type. Aside from his build, he was mildly attractive, being Italian with jet black hair. But his most impressive feature was his shockingly green eyes fringed with the longest, darkest eyelashes I had ever seen.

As time passed and after Mon Homme's return to rehab, I focused on work. I loved selling granite and my boss was easier to work with, now that I knew the basics. I also appreciated the sober attention he offered and thought about his playful laugh, wondering if we could have fun together.

With this thought in mind, the next time he asked me to dinner, I agreed, and Rebound Man became my occasional companion. We started going out, squeezing in dates between our hectic work schedules.

We had been on a few dates, when one evening I noticed his wandering eye. I had taken the time to get ready for the evening and knew I looked good, even if he didn't see it. My hair was curled into sexy, flowing waves and I was wearing a beautiful, silver-blue dress that highlighted my eyes.

The dress was a classy, feminine delight with spaghetti straps and a draped cowl neckline. It kissed my curves and caressed my thighs, stopping an inch above the knees.

To complete the picture, I wore bone and ice-blue stilettos with silver heels that complemented the dainty silver necklace and earrings. Having addressed all details, I believed my efforts were a success.

"I have to wonder," I said, as we were seated at our table. "How can you be on a date with me, yet staring at the girl over there?"

"Whattaya mean?"

"Seriously? You've been asking me out, and this is what you do? Have you looked at your date tonight? What about her makes you want to stare at *that* girl?" I asked, sitting back in the booth.

"I dunno what you're talkin' 'bout. You're being paranoid."

"No, not paranoid. Just curious," I said, reaching for the menu. "It's no big deal if we go out. You're the one pursuing me. But it's one thing to look, and another to stare. It's rude and disrespectful, regardless of our status," I said, setting the menu aside.

"Oh, here we go! A lecture I don't need. Sorry I noticed her. D'ya want me ta never look at another woman?"

"Don't be ridiculous, you know what I'm saying. Don't blow things out of proportion to make me out to be something I'm not, just because I called you out. If this is how you're going to be, then please take me home," I said, starting to rise.

"No, I'm sorry," he said, reaching for my hand and gesturing to the seat. "Please. I guess I was just checkin' her out. Old habits die hard," he said with a nervous laugh.

"Well, at least you're finally being honest," I said, taking my seat.

The server arrived and we ordered our dinner. With that moment behind us, we had a decent time and finished our evening.

I thought about it after dinner and knew it was irrelevant to me if we dated. I could take it or leave it; I had enough on my plate. Dating him was merely a distraction from the monotony of work and my wounded heart.

We continued seeing each other and his attention span improved. It was fun at first, as always, and we worked well together. As a team, the clients loved working with us and the result was both professional as well as personal, making us a desired contractor within our field.

With both of us working seven days a week, the only time we had to spend together was in the evenings. By the end of my day, I was ready for something low-key, making our evening events of dinner and a movie the accepted norm.

We were having dinner at his place one night, when he brought up his past. At first it was strange, because I hadn't thought about his relationship with his ex-wife enough to be curious. But as he disclosed a few details, certain questions began taking shape at the back of my mind.

"She was a physician's assistant and always whined about being tired," he said, pouring two glasses of wine. "We never went out and she did nothin' 'round the house. It got old being married ta someone who didn't care 'bout the responsibilities of a woman."

"What do you mean, 'responsibilities of a woman'?" I asked, sensing distinct chauvinism as I took a bite of my salad.

"Ya know, she's supposed ta cook, clean, shop. That stuff. It was ridiculous," he said, rolling his eyes.

"Was she alright?" I asked, setting my fork down and focusing on the conversation. "Was she sick? She sounds too young to be so tired. Was she a student?"

"No. She just did nothin'."

"So what happened? Why did you get divorced?"

"She tried ta commit suicide one day," he said, without the slightest hint of emotion. Cracking the shell of his lobster, he tore the meat away and cast the shell aside.

"That doesn't sound right," I said, shaking my head. "The signs were there. Didn't you encourage her to see a doctor or something?"

"She worked with one and shoulda known better," he said, shrugging his shoulders nonchalantly while slurping the buttery lobster from his fork.

While finishing my bite, I thought about what he said. I was appalled by his lack of empathy and confused by the conversation.

She was no longer in the picture and he was obviously detached and unaffected with their details, so why did he bring her up? I wasn't sure what his angle was, but if it was to gain sympathy for himself or to find out if I would cook and clean for him, he would soon be disappointed.

"Well, usually people in the midst of a situation rarely recognize they need help," I said. "It's sad. I'm sorry it ended like that, but hopefully she's doing better. Let's finish dinner and find a movie to watch."

"Yeah, good idea," he said, appearing relieved that the conversation was over.

Maybe the conversation was, but I was skeptical she was at fault for everything. Reflecting on the bit he volunteered and his lack of emotion, I wondered if he had something to do with her overall state of mind.

Although I was uncertain, I believed I would eventually discover the truth.

Chapter 31

Batten Down the Hatches

After coming on board to work for Rebound Man, I worked diligently as an ambitious contributor to the company. I immediately took on the task of creating new presentation materials, redesigned and updated the company's sales contract, and also pursued and acquired wholesale accounts.

I established relationships with anyone and everyone in the industry that I could, and began building a reputation as someone who stood behind her word. Having been raised in a business, I understood the value of excellent customer service and this was right up my alley.

Approximately five months after starting, I began seeing tangible progress for my efforts. Several wholesale accounts had requested countless site visits, quotes, and samples without awarding any contracts, and I delivered. I survived the preliminary test, and now the clients were sending me their business on a constant flow.

Incidentally, and ironically, the increase in business from my sales spurred a distinct chill with Rebound Man. My paychecks were steadily growing and it provoked him. He claimed I was overpaid, conveniently dismissing the months I had worked for minimal (if any) income. Commencing with my growing success at work, our relationship rapidly escalated into another dramatic adventure.

His resentment manifested itself in many ways. He muttered about having to pay me, supply samples from his slabs, and answer work-related questions. And of course, his toxic attitude hastily seeped into our personal relationship.

"Can you believe how many jobs we've landed from Next of Kin Cabinets?" I asked playfully one afternoon. "I've worked diligently for them since day one, and it's rewarding to finally receive some contracts."

"Yeah, good for you. Tomorrow they could change their mind and decide they don't wanna work with ya no more."

"Don't be silly! Who wouldn't want to work with this?" I asked, twirling around with two samples in my hands. I laughed as I danced my way over to him and kissed him on the cheek.

He pulled back and rolled his eyes. "You're ridiculous. They're not workin' with *you* because of *you*. They're workin' with *us* because of the product and price," he said, slamming a drawer as he walked past me.

"Well, maybe so," I said, raising my chin and putting the samples away. "But you hadn't won them over before I started, and you said you wanted them the most. So, please *do not* pretend I have nothing to do with the business they're giving you. On that note and with your attitude, I'm going home. Goodnight," I said, heading for the door.

"Yeah, whatever," I heard him grunt as the door closed behind me.

I continued working without going to the office for a few days, avoiding his mood swings. I loved my job and did not want it to suffer because he had a huge ego and could barely squeeze through the door with it.

Over the following week, he called several times for silly reasons. We discussed a few jobs and then I would end the conversation, remaining aloof. I knew he was checking my temperature to see where he stood, but I was unwilling to reveal anything definitive.

Several days later, I met a designer at the shop to select her slab. When I arrived, he was cool and kept his distance. I had arranged for him to meet my client and when she arrived, he became two people at the same time.

"Hi Annelle, thanks for coming in," I said as she approached the counter. "This is the manager, Rebound Man."

"It's nice to meet you," he said, oozing with charm. "Let me show you our inventory." He shook her hand while maintaining eye contact with me.

"Thank you, I'd love to see it. You know, you have the most beautiful eyes," she said to him as we all moved into the warehouse.

"Thank you," he replied, smiling his cheesy grin.

I noticed how he changed his manner of speaking with clients as we began touring the facility and had to smile inside. Keeping it to myself, I attempted to learn more about the job to better understand what she wanted.

"What colors are you working with?" I asked.

"I'm working with all naturals. I could go in a variety of directions, but prefer the beige and cream family."

"Let's start with those colors," he said, leading her in the opposite direction. "What's your project?"

"I need a top for a Victorian vanity. It'll be small, but the focal point of the powder room."

"That sounds nice," I said. "Have you chosen your faucet?"

"She doesn't need her faucet yet," he said, turning and glaring at me. "She can choose her granite first."

"I know. I asked in case there was a particular tone to consider."

"I'm glad you asked, Kendyl. I have a spectacular, oil-rubbed bronze faucet. If possible, I want to find a piece with that color throughout," she said, appearing oblivious to the power tug-of-war going on around her.

"That's perfect. We have several slabs that would be stunning with your combination. Let's go over here," I said. But as I turned to lead her toward another section, Rebound Man hastily stepped between us.

"Kendyl," he said while putting his hand up to stop us, "we have several new slabs you haven't seen yet. *I'll* make sure she sees them."

"Great, I'd like to see them, too. Please lead the way," I said, waving him forward. Refusing to be ousted from my own appointment, I turned my attention back to my client. "I can't wait to see it finished, Annelle. Your work is impressive and I know you'll choose something gorgeous."

We continued through the warehouse, and she eventually chose her slab. As I wrote up the contract, Rebound Man came up behind me. Looking over my shoulder, he instructed me to do it right and adjust the total.

Although we were behind the counter where Annelle could not see what we were doing, he spoke loud enough for her to hear his reprimand.

Shooting him an inquisitive look, I asked as nicely as possible how to figure the cost, because I was unaware of any price changes.

He sighed, rolled his eyes, and snatched the pen from my grasp. He haughtily crossed a heavy line through the total, reducing it by ten percent.

"Like that," he said, forcibly placing the pen on the counter. "You'll need patience with her, Annelle. She still doesn't know what she's doing."

I rewrote the contract and explained the details to her. She signed it and presented her check for the deposit. I took both items and placed them in the file and handed it to Rebound Man. After he assigned an installation date for the project, I walked her out, thanked her for her business, and returned to the office.

"What was that about?" I asked, now that we were alone.

"What?"

"You want to play that card again? How do you think it looks when you belittle me, especially in front of others?"

"I dunno what you're talkin' 'bout," he said, sporting an arrogant smirk and adjusting the files. "She thinks I'm amazing. I just gave her a great deal on a small job that's gonna be a waste of my time ta do."

"Really? You think people don't care that you're disrespectful to your staff? And, this isn't just about business. You shouldn't treat me like that, period," I said, my temper rising as I gathered my things to leave. "By the way, we won't be going out anymore. I've had enough of your condescending remarks, and we both know this won't be the last of them."

"Whattaya talkin' 'bout?" he asked, his smirk disappearing as he gave me his full attention. "I don't speak down ta ya. You're always makin' things up!"

"See? You refuse to admit it, and I refuse to accept it. I'll stay on as a rep, but you won't see me unless I have to come in for something," I said, heading for the exit.

"You're not makin' sense. You're throwin' away a good thing," he said, following me.

"No, I'm not. I know this is good for you, but it doesn't work for me."

I kept walking without looking back and let the door close behind me to finalize my statement. After dating him for a few months, I understood his motives and no longer wished to be involved with him.

Rebound Man was a classic case of a controlling, jealous man when the raw truth of his nature was exposed. The need to control everything between us, including my income, became evident as he manipulated situations to undermine my character and reputation.

Appearing professional, congenial, and charming to others, he managed to deceive them. But when things did not go his way, the smooth, elegant façade dissipated to reveal what was hidden beneath, and now it was time to batten down the hatches.

I quickly discovered after ending our personal relationship that he could not separate the business. His fragile, super-sized ego would not be defeated by a woman he could not have and control and he would carry his grudge to the finish line.

The following weeks were challenging. His attitude oozed into every aspect of my work, resulting in health-oriented side effects for me.

I was fine on Monday, but by Tuesday afternoon a headache would set in. It persisted daily, intensifying into a full-blown migraine by midday Wednesday. Thursday and Friday were a blur as I struggled to function through the pain, barely able to concentrate on my work.

Separated from any communication with him over the weekend, the migraine subsided and I was in top form by Monday morning. This pattern persisted for five weeks. Focused on my clients, I was unaware of the underlying cause of the debilitating headaches.

However, I eventually realized the problem stemmed from the anxiety of dealing with him and how he manipulated the results of my work. The elevated, intense stress depleted my blood sugar faster than normal, sending me straight into a migraine tailspin.

Thankfully, although I would not appreciate it immediately, he would force an end to our business relationship. Determined to defeat me, he inflicted as much harm as possible to my professional reputation.

Even though it meant jeopardizing business, my clients' projects became his target. I was working closely with an interior designer when he decided to create a complete upheaval, proving nothing was off limits.

The job was to create and install a massive, 3" Bullnose, Black Fusion granite bar top. It would be the center of attention and rightly so, with its commanding, impressive edge and waves of black, copper, and pearl hues. The flow of the rich colors accentuated by the overhead lights would ensure the top could stand alone as a piece of artwork.

To protect the wall from the wet bar, I designed an intriguing backsplash that included copper tiles spaced intermittently to complement the granite. The combination would make a stunning first impression.

When I presented the samples and drawings to the homeowner, she was thrilled and gave me a hug. She thanked me for bringing it all together and was eager to see the finished project. This was my job: seeing a vision for the client, making it happen, and giving them something to love every time they looked at it.

I drew up the contract, copied the drawings with detailed notes for the fabricators, and submitted them to the interior designer for client approval. After receiving approval, I turned the drawings and the deposit over to Rebound Man, following company protocol as always.

Simultaneously, I advised him of the size of the job, knowing it would take longer to fabricate. He glanced at the drawings and wrote the installation date on the schedule. I called the client to let them know when we would install, and everything was complete on my end.

Three days prior to the installation, I called Rebound Man to check on the job's status. "Good morning," I said cheerfully when he answered the phone. "Are we on schedule to install Monday for At Home Interiors? I want to confirm with them today."

"Install what?"

"The Black Fusion bar top and tile backsplash I submitted three weeks ago."

"I dunno what you're talkin' 'bout. Never heard of it," he said, sounding pleased.

"I submitted the file to you personally," I said, patiently playing along while rolling my eyes. "We discussed the job in detail, including extra time for fabrication, and you scheduled the install."

"Well, I'm not responsible for your jobs. *You* are. You'd better call and tell 'em we won't be there Monday. It'll take three days ta make. You'd better find a way ta make 'em happy," he said, hanging up.

I knew he was trying to upset me and it was working because he was messing with my livelihood as well as my reputation. I can handle a lot of personal attacks, but when you mess with these two things, a part of me roars that is otherwise seldom heard.

Although annoyed with his game, I was determined to maintain a level of professionalism for my client, and called him back. "I'll be happy to call the client, but what date and time should I tell them?" I asked politely.

"Tell 'em we'll install Wednesday mornin'."

"Nine o'clock, correct?"

"Yeah," he said, hanging up again.

Sighing with disgust, I dialed the interior designer, hoping for a peaceful interaction. She answered on the first ring.

"Hi Sara, this is Kendyl. I'm sorry to bother you, but there's an issue with the bar top and we need to reschedule the installation. Could you please ask your client if Wednesday at nine works?"

"Sure. I'll try to catch them before the weekend and let you know."

"Thanks, I appreciate your understanding," I said, letting her go.

She called back a few minutes later. "Yes, we're on for Wednesday morning. She wasn't thrilled with the inconvenience, but we're all set."

"Okay, thank you. I'll tell the shop. Have a great weekend, Sara."

After confirming with her, I called the shop. Rebound Man answered and I told him we were on for Wednesday, and then continued with my day.

The following Tuesday morning, I went to the office to review the status of the fabrication and to ensure we were on target for the next day's installation. He was in the shop when I arrived and barely glanced in my direction when I walked in.

"Good morning. Are we on track to install tomorrow morning?" I asked.

"No. Tell 'em it'll be Thursday."

"Why? This job has already been postponed once. This is ridiculous. What's the problem *this* time?"

"A piece broke tryin' ta meet *your* deadline."

"Sure it did. And don't forget who sets the deadlines around here. I'll call them again, but this is pathetic. They deserve better service than you're providing," I said, reaching for my cell phone and heading outside.

I paced the parking lot while dialing Sara's number, anticipating an unpleasant conversation. Once again, she answered promptly.

"Hi Sara, this is Kendyl. I regret having to tell you this, but a piece of the top broke during fabrication. We won't be able to install until Thursday. I can't apologize enough for these delays."

"This is unheard of!" she shouted. "This is both unprofessional and unacceptable. I want to talk to your boss!"

"I don't blame you. Please call him and see what he can do to amend the situation," I said, providing his cell phone number.

I returned to the shop and told Rebound Man she would be calling him. He was furious with me, but before he could finish the verbal assault he had launched into, his phone rang. It was Sara.

Setting his temper aside, he smoothly switched gears, sounding calm and in control when he answered the phone. I could hear her elevated tone from where I stood and she was giving him an earful. As I listened, I heard him twist himself out of being the villain and into the hero.

"Yes, I understand how you feel. I know she's been working with you and obviously forgot to put the job on the schedule. We didn't even know about it," he said, watching me closely as a hint of a smile came to his lips.

His eyes were sparkling as he sat and put his feet up on his desk, rocking back to a casual, reclined position. Flipping a pen between two fingers, he carried on, enjoying the drama he had created.

"I know, and I agree," he said. "This is extremely unprofessional. I don't appreciate the pickle it put us in, either. I'll have a talk with her."

The conversation continued, and although her words were muffled, I knew she was not placated with only my reprimand. Rebound Man's eyes never left me as he listened to her argument.

"Yes, of course. I agree. I'll be happy to take $500.00 off the job," he said, in between her ranting. He was silent while she continued, apparently still not satisfied with the promise of my scolding and a decent discount.

"I understand. I'll let her know, and look forward to working with you in the future," he said as the conversation came to a close.

He was still wearing his famous evil smirk when he hung up the phone and tossed it on the desk. He was clearly pleased with how his plan was coming together as he stood to give me the news.

"You're off the job," he said, dropping the pen next to the phone and tucking in his shirt. "She don't wanna work with ya no more. She said you're unprofessional and refused ta pay full price. I had ta give her the discount just ta shut her up."

Silently, I gathered my purse and glanced around the shop to make sure I had everything. Turning to leave, I crossed the showroom floor and headed for the door.

"I'll drop off my files when I pick up my check next week," I said over my shoulder while pushing the door open. I exited the shop without looking back and went home, surprisingly relieved.

Although I knew the end was near, I never imagined he would sabotage a job to ruin me. He could have let me go and ended everything without jeopardizing a contract with a client. Instead, he chose this blatant attack to make his point.

He destroyed my name and reputation with Sara for his revenge. In addition, I was disappointed I would never see the finished project and the happiness it brought the homeowner when she saw it.

He completed the installation and when I picked up the check, I noticed a hefty amount was missing. Despite dreading another conversation with him, I knew I had to ask about the missing funds before leaving.

He was gloating when he informed me the deductions were for fabrication errors as well as the discount provided to appease the client. He stated the fabricators were rushed and initially cut the granite incorrectly, which doubled the cost in material.

He was vividly proud of his clever revenge and relished telling me I was paying for the additional job costs. He announced that he was tired of having to cover expenses for mishaps with the jobs, and someone else could start chipping in.

I listened to his explanation for not paying my full commission and refused to give him more satisfaction by arguing with him. Instead, I promptly quipped we would meet on legal turf to resolve the matter and left before he could respond.

I started the car and revved the engine, making sure all eight cylinders emphasized my strong attitude. Shifting into first gear, I rolled out of his parking lot for the last time, with him and his shop becoming miniature in my rearview mirror. Naturally, I replayed the entire ordeal on my way home, including the job setbacks he initiated.

I knew his argument pertaining to others sharing costs was irrational because, if for no other reason, they were not the owners. In this case, it was truly absurd, because his vindictive agenda was the cause for the additional expenses, not me. Had he removed his precious ego from the situation, the job would have been completed on time with profit, and the client would have been spared unnecessary frustration.

Even though he appeared to be narcissistic, I was flabbergasted by his course of action. I realized he did not care about upsetting everyone because he believed it would only reflect poorly on me. It was illogical, but he had been willing to lose a client for his revenge.

Luckily for him, he was able to convince Sara that I was at fault and spare his reputation with her, at least for the time being. Therefore, he probably thought the only loss created by his superiority was the one he passed on to me, which made his plan a complete success.

However, I was not convinced it would stick. I believed I would eventually prevail and he would be forced to absorb the costs of his own pride.

It was not over, even though he was accustomed to pushing people around and getting away with it. I was not meek and submissive, nor was I afraid of him.

Not this girl.

Chapter 32

Karma

I hired an attorney through a friend of mine that afternoon. He requested a meeting with Rebound Man, who readily agreed. According to the attorney and as expected, Jake would not be present. The date was set for the following week.

I wanted to be prepared for the confrontation and gathered copies of contracts, cashed paychecks, and notes from jobs. I clipped them together and slid the last paycheck, still uncashed, under the clip and on top of the paperwork. I placed it all in the file and waited for our meeting.

The following week, I went to the attorney's office, arriving twenty minutes early. Rebound Man strutted in ten minutes later. When he saw me, a smirk of satisfaction appeared. He maintained his expression as we were ushered to our seats in the conference room.

Thankfully, the attorney joined us immediately. Between his prompt arrival and the efficiency of his staff, the two of us were never left alone, preventing opportunity for an exchange of any kind.

Although the attorney knew the details of my claim, I placed the file in the chair next to me, in case I needed it for reference. Rebound Man also had a file and presented it to him, taking the seat opposite me. He sat back, crossed his arms over his chest, and gave me an upward nod while sporting his evil grin.

The attorney greeted us as he took his seat at the head of the table. He took a few minutes to look everything over and appeared a bit confused.

After his review, he asked Rebound Man why we were meeting.

Evidently, he was planning to countersue for damages I had caused (hence the grin). The damages were to include the loss of clientele and their future business. According to him, my clients canceled their contracts and requested the return of their deposits when they discovered I no longer worked for the company.

This last detail wound up totaling a sum of more than $10,000.00, and he was holding me accountable. He claimed I was working for a competitor and took the accounts, which caused my attorney to pause.

"Kendyl, have you taken up a position with a competitor and pursued your clients?" he asked, looking at the documents before him.

"No, I haven't," I said, shaking my head. "I've moved on in a different direction."

"I see. Then in that case, it's impossible for you to have done what he is accusing you of."

His brow furrowed as he concentrated on the details and addressed Rebound Man. He was piecing everything together in his mind, speaking slowly while forming his thoughts.

"I don't understand, sir," he said, looking at the paperwork while rubbing his forehead. "I know certain clients wanted to work with her so badly that they canceled their contracts when she left. But she wasn't working in the industry anymore. Plus, she'd made you a lot of money. So, why did you let her go?" he asked, shaking his head.

The evil grin disappeared instantly from Rebound Man's face and was replaced with a priceless expression, silently acknowledging the validity of the question. Before he could respond, the attorney continued, informing each of us of our options.

"You do realize, don't you, that if she takes you to court, she will most assuredly be awarded the full amount of her request? I strongly urge you to settle today."

Then he shifted his gaze to me and said, "If you take this to court, Kendyl, be advised that your court date will be in several months, taking you well into next year. Obviously, it's up to you."

I was thrilled with his suggestion and grateful for his advice. I wanted everything related to Rebound Man whisked out of my life as soon as possible and preferred to wrap it up immediately. Time is too precious and I was too busy. Going to court a year later to rehash the mess and deal with him again would create unproductive stress. It simply was not worth it.

Previously anticipating settling for less than requested, I had set the amount higher than necessary to meet the debt he owed. Therefore, I happily negotiated a number to clear his debt and my expenses, and provide a little extra for tolerating him. The revised amount allowed us to settle that afternoon, preventing further delay.

I was relieved to put it all behind me when I left the attorney's office. I replayed the meeting in my mind and realized how rewarding it was to have things work out in my favor, despite his attempts to ruin me further.

Karma has a way of shedding light on one's intentions and revealing the truth, but we are seldom fortunate enough to witness it firsthand. This little gift was my bonus that day.

Several years later, he phoned.

"Kendyl, it's Rebound Man."

"What do you want?"

"I just wanna tell ya that, as far as I'm concerned, there's no bad blood 'tween us."

"Really?" I asked, stifling the sudden urge to laugh. "Don't you think after what you said to and about me and what you put me through, that *I* should be the one to make that decision? Don't think you're doing me any favors."

And before I could take my next breath, I hung up. It felt great to be the one to cut him off after his previous hang ups and snide remarks.

Although I should not have been surprised, I could not believe he had the audacity to call and act like he was blessing me. In addition, being well aware of his arrogance, I was skeptical his motive was to make amends.

Maybe the old version of me would have been more gullible, but not the slightly wiser version. Regardless, I did not care what he wanted because I knew I wanted nothing to do with him.

However, even though I have no fondness for him and think his character is severely lacking, I can appreciate the experiences that came from the relationship.

He provided exposure to a career that I previously had no intention of pursuing and for me, it was fun and creative. I enjoyed the clients, jobs, and satisfaction when an installation was a success.

As for the personal experience, it led to a deeper understanding of how stress affects my health. I also learned to avoid romantic relationships with employers going forward.

In addition, I wish to thank Rebound Man for inadvertently reminding me of the importance of self-respect and knowing where to draw the line.

And so, from you Rebound Man, I steal back my self-respect, something I understand most pirates like to take from others. I also proudly steal back the opportunity to be successful in business as a woman, despite your chauvinistic beliefs.

As for you? Well, I believe Karma has your number.

I think I'll leave it at that.

Chapter 33

Pillaged by a Scurvy Dog

While I was dating Rebound Man, I started searching for an investment property. I was considering either raw land to hold on to or a place to rehab. I wanted to do something different and constructive with some money, and thought the adventure would be fun.

In the mix of my search and after finalizing the chaos with him, I started dating another man, referred to herein as Leech. One who quickly revealed himself to be a true scurvy dog, this pirate is reviewed because he indirectly played a supporting role, which is included here for the sake of the story.

Our interlude was brief and admittedly, made no sense at all from the perspective of a romantic relationship. A mere two and a half months from the first flirtation to the last slamming of the door, there was little between us from the beginning.

We connected at the beach. I was drawn to him because he was free-spirited and relaxed which, on the surface, seemed to be what I needed after the drama of Rebound Man. Everything was light and casual between us, and I welcomed being in a relationship free of stress and anxiety.

During one of our conversations about things we wanted to do, I shared my desire to buy a fixer-upper. In response, he mentioned his construction experience and convinced me he not only could do the work, but also wanted to take on the project with me. It was his willingness to assist that gave me the confidence to proceed with the purchase.

We struck a deal wherein I would front the financial costs and he would invest the sweat equity doing the physical work, splitting the profits in the end. After locating a house I thought was a perfect contender, I showed it to him for his input.

He agreed the structure was solid and the remodeling process would be an easy undertaking. Thrilled to have found the perfect project and a partner to help complete the task, I bought it without hesitation.

The first week after taking possession, Leech began working on the house. I was pleased with his ambition and excited to have the project underway, convinced it would be finished in a few months.

A few days after he started the demolition work, he had a request. We were at my place and I was emptying the dishwasher, when he joined me in the kitchen.

"I have to move out of Ryan's place," he said, resting his long, lean surfer's body against the counter. "He's getting married and I don't have anywhere to go. We're dating anyway, so how 'bout I move in with you?"

"Sure, okay. When do you need to move out?"

"By the weekend. He just told me last night."

"Wow, that's short notice. I know you're looking for more work, but you'll still have to contribute for expenses and groceries," I said, putting the last of the dishes in the cabinet.

"I'll pay you, I promise," he said, taking me into his arms and pulling me close. His dark-brown eyes were soft and playful. "It'll be great. We'll have more time together because I'll be right here," he whispered.

"Yes, you will," I said quietly with a wink. "But right now, I need to eat, so let's focus on dinner." Pulling away, I took the salad out of the refrigerator and asked him to set it on the table.

Honestly, I did not see that coming. But at the same time, others had lived with me in the past and I didn't think twice about it. Even though we had known each other a short time, we were involved in an investment project together and it didn't occur to me to refuse.

After dinner, we discussed how to rearrange things to make room for his few belongings and by the end of the weekend, he was settled in. Our daily routine took us each our separate ways. I went to work and he told me he went to work or looking for more employment (depending on his work schedule), and then afterward, to work at the house.

In the beginning, this pattern made sense. We still found time to be together and would go rollerblading, biking, diving, or to the beach. We discussed what was going on, the progress he said he was making at the house, as well as other tidbits of the day.

One afternoon, I had extra time and stopped by the house with a few items I wanted to include in the job. He had said earlier that he was going to be working there for several hours, and I wanted to surprise him and help out. His car was not in the driveway when I arrived, and I assumed he was shopping for supplies. I unloaded the car and went inside.

I was wrong. I toured the house and saw nothing had changed since the first time we were there, a week prior. Disgusted with him for lying and myself for believing him, I locked up and headed home.

During the drive, I reflected on the recent past and what had transpired. I recalled how he started complaining about working all the time right after moving in. He hated his job and resented being restricted to working construction, yet he also hated the idea of getting a new job to improve his situation.

While whining about his work, he also confessed he was unable to maintain his expenses. Although I heard his woes, I was preoccupied with my own financial obligations and therefore, did not heed the warnings from the red flags. Instead, I thought I needed his help and went with the flow, assuming he was working on the house like he said.

I also realized how quickly he acclimated to living in my home and how comfortable he was in his new surroundings. He knew I trusted him and began acting as though there were no boundaries between us.

It was within the first month that, after explaining his dire financial situation and why he could not afford to pay his rent, Leech asked for help paying his child support. Foolishly, I agreed and gave him the money, believing he would pay it back.

This act of generosity seemed to convince him that I was hooked. He let his guard down, allowing himself to relax and be exactly who he was. It appeared as though the flood gates were opened and his true nature came rushing forth, one instance after the other, revealing his real intentions.

I remember one weekend when he had his beautiful five-year-old daughter and we were going to take her to the beach. When the morning arrived and before it was time to leave, I told him I had a headache and the heat would make it worse. If it subsided, then I would join them.

Agitated with my decision, he placed the absolutely best part of himself in her car seat and off they went. When their day ended, they returned and he was still perturbed.

"What's wrong?" I asked.

"What's *wrong*?" he asked, shooting me an angry look. He was pacing back and forth in the living room, opening and closing his fists. "What's wrong is that you didn't come and didn't call to tell me you weren't coming! *That's* what's wrong!" he yelled, violently jabbing his finger at the air in front of me.

"Why are you upset?" I asked calmly, trying not to upset his daughter while brushing her hair. "I told you if I changed my mind, I'd come. Besides, you leave your phone in the car, so what difference does it make that I didn't call?"

"Because I had to ask someone else to watch her, so I could go surfing!"

What a jerk, I thought. He had this delightfully amazing daughter, who was a gift of fun and adoration, yet all he could think of was how to rid himself of his responsibility to her for his own playtime.

"You're kidding me, right?" I asked, putting her hair in a ponytail.

"No, I'm not *kidding* you! I had to ask my friend's wife to watch her. I can't believe you put me in that position!"

"You're ridiculous, Leech. She's *your* daughter. If you think I'm here to be a babysitter-on-demand, think again. It's pathetic that when you have her, you push her onto someone else. She deserves better," I said, wishing I could take her away from him.

He huffed and stomped off, slapping the wall on his way out. Silence set in as he retreated to the bathroom to take a shower, slamming the door behind him. I embraced the peace and hugged his lovely daughter, thinking she must be used to seeing him angry because she appeared unaffected.

We went to the kitchen and fixed dinner together. When it was ready, we sat and had a delightful time giggling and sharing our macaroni and cheese before he returned to smother us with his sulking. As the weekend wound down, his temper cooled and he returned to being civil.

By the end of the following week, yet another incident followed. He returned home late one evening, having forgotten to call. In case that wasn't suspicious enough after his previous claim against me, he was not wearing his watch. I noticed this, because I gave it to him and he never took it off.

In the middle of our brief relationship, and before I realized I was being played, Leech had his birthday. I love birthdays and finding the perfect gift is important to me. After spending considerable time searching, I found a handsome, waterproof watch he could wear while diving.

"Where's your watch?" I asked, when I looked up from my puzzle.

"Oh . . . uh, I must've left it at Ryan's," he said, flushing and grabbing his wrist.

"Why did you take it off?"

"I was helping with some fish in the aquarium, if it's any of your business!"

"Ah, yes. It's important to remove a waterproof watch approved for diving up to 150′ when you stick your arm in a fish tank."

I turned my attention back to the puzzle, thinking it was most definitely my business. After all, he was living in my home, pretending to be my boyfriend. Naturally, I wanted to know where that watch was, and why. I wasn't sure what it was, but I knew something in his story did not line up.

I will admit that I was naïve of his intentions when we met, but I was not a complete idiot. Therefore, while he was making up stories, I was putting the pieces together.

At this point, we had been together for two months and it was time to do my typical investigation before sending him out the door. I continued checking up on him to gather facts and strengthen my argument. And, although I knew he was not working at the house, I chose to pretend to be ignorant of that detail for the time being.

Every day, he said he was going to the other house to work. Therefore, I satisfied my suspicion by going to the beach every afternoon to watch him surf and live the good life at my expense.

I discovered everything he told me was a lie.

In truth, he was lazy and dedicated to being a beach bum. He specialized in manipulating others and playing off their sympathy. Convincing them he was a victim repeatedly dealt a bad hand, he used them to pay for his existence for as long as he could. Now, he was using me.

It became evident when my friend of many years summed it up for me, explaining how he apparently mistook my kindness as weakness. Yes, his plan worked at first, but in the end, he underestimated me. When his motive became clear and after I pieced the details of his story together, I was determined to deal him a brand-new hand.

However, rather than confront him (because he would only lie and it no longer mattered), I used the information as motivation to move on. I knew better than to waste my time and energy on someone who blatantly abused my generosity.

My analysis complete, I now understood the situation. And, although he owed me money, I was not interested in collecting on his debt because I knew this, too, would be futile. In the end, the financial loss would be a small price to pay. But right now, he needed to leave before he cost me another dime.

It was time to take action.

He returned from another sun-drenched, glorious day at the beach. While he showered, I reclaimed my keys from his key ring, stashed them in a drawer, and then gathered his belongings. This task was a snap because pursuing the lifestyle of a roaming beach bum naturally prevented him from accumulating many possessions.

When he came out of the shower, I asked him to take the garbage out before dinner. I quickly found his shower toiletries and dirty laundry and tossed them in the bag. Meeting him at the door, I handed his things to him and told him to leave.

He was shocked, his expression revealing everything. It was obvious he did not expect to be evicted. He started yelling and causing a loud, obnoxious scene as the door closed on his bright-red, angry face.

He shouted accusations and threats pertaining to how much money I owed him for his work. He paced like a madman, occasionally pounding on the door with his fists. I ignored his tirade and closed the blinds, shutting him out of my life forever.

After approximately twenty minutes of yelling and screaming, I heard his car door slam. Revving the engine, he peeled out of the driveway.

With peace restored, it was time to relax. I headed to the bathroom to take a hot soak in the tub and shake off the day. I was relieved it was over and hoped to never see him again. I didn't know where he went, nor did I care, as long as it was away from me.

While I soaked, I thought about his accusation that I owed him money. I found it interesting that he had the nerve to claim anything of the sort. His work at the house consisted of only cutting holes in one wall, nothing else. In addition, he lived rent-free for several weeks, *and* I paid his child support for him. Ah yes, but I owed him.

Considering his skewed logic, I could see why he thought he was always getting a raw deal. Rounding out my thoughts on the topic, I was pleased to be moving forward without him and finished my bath in peace.

A few days later, I visited the other property and discovered he had broken in and camped out. I found his belongings (minus the surfboard), tucked away in a closet and decided he no longer needed them.

I loaded his stuff into my car, locked up the house, and left. On the way home, I located a dumpster in a back alley and disposed of everything.

Naturally, this led to another visit to my doorstep, where his final pleas for another chance fell on apathetic ears through exterior walls. After numerous unanswered phone calls and threats, he gave up and disappeared.

I refused to be pillaged twice by this pirate. Although he never had any chance of stealing my soul (or my heart), he had literally stolen through my kindness and generosity.

Through reflection, I see that I was oblivious to how my ambition and genuine desire to pursue a goal, served as an opportunity for him to have a better lifestyle at my expense. He understood what to say to win my trust, and it worked for him. And, before realizing he was conning me at every turn, I believed his story.

So that was, with respect to the investment property, plan A.

Admittedly, I was a novice and made my share of mistakes. But believe it or not, Leech served a purpose.

Somehow, I unwittingly convinced myself I needed the security of a partner to proceed with my dream to remodel a house. When he claimed he knew construction and volunteered to work with me, he wound up providing what I thought I needed, even though he was a fraud in the end.

I know now that I did not need you for anything, Leech.

In truth, I know that somewhere deep down, I always knew it. And for indirectly helping me to realize it, I say thank you.

Chapter 34

Given Quarter

It was time to move on to plan B, now that plan A was null and void. Plan B originally consisted of completing the house alone. I begged contractors to show up for the work previously agreed on but to no avail, leaving the project to rest entirely on my shoulders.

Relentlessly pursuing the goal, I spent most of my time either working on the house, or at the local hardware store gathering tools and supplies to finish the task at hand. It was yet another day, when I stopped to pick up more supplies.

While I was making my way up and down the aisles, I was approached by a man I knew from when I was a project manager. He was an executive at an affiliated company at the time, and I had not seen him in years.

"Kendyl? Is that you?"

"Yes? Oh my goodness! How are you doing after all these years? What are you doing here?" I asked, unable to hide my surprise.

"I have a plumbing issue in my guest bathroom I need to fix."

"That's great you can do your own handyman chores! I wish I could. I admit, I'm a bit jealous."

"Yes, it saves a lot of money. So, what have you been up to? What are you doing here?" he asked, scanning my basket.

"Currently, I'm working on remodeling a house, which is why I'm here pretty much every other day. It's not going as planned, but it's coming along, slowly but surely."

"Really? I love that stuff. Let me know if I can help," he said, providing his phone number.

I must confess that remodeling a house was not on my list of skills and my progress was slower than a confused turtle crossing a road. Therefore, I eagerly welcomed the friendly assistance and hastily accepted his offer.

Two days later, we met at the house and he loved it. Seeing the same potential I saw, he wanted to start working as soon as possible. We coordinated our schedules and within the blink of an eye, I was given quarter with a new partner.

We went to work without delay, determined to create the cutest place we could. We gutted the kitchen, tore down walls and built new ones, replaced appliances and cabinets, scrubbed showers and floors, painted walls and ceilings, tamped sand, laid brick, and even planted flowers. We worked well together and the project quickly evolved into more of a fun, social event, rather than a chore.

A year after purchasing the house, it was finished. It was the freshest, cleanest house on the street and positively adorable, promising to be a great find for the new owners. It was time to put it back on the market for sale.

I listed the house with a friend of mine who worked in real estate, and it sold four days later. She said it was the quickest sale she had ever made, and I confessed I was glad it was off my plate.

I called my remodeling partner and told him the good news, thanking him again for his assistance. When the closing was complete, we met for coffee, talked about how the house turned out, and I paid him the balance of what I owed.

When he walked me to my car that afternoon, he asked me to dinner.

Chapter 35

The Seadog and His Lassie

As I sift through my pieces of eight, I find the tale of an older pirate and his lassie which begs to be told. I, being the lassie, can assure you that what follows may leave you altered, but tell the tale I must in keeping with the rest of the story.

The course of order for a pirate such as this must certainly demand a taunting visit to Davy Jones's locker to set him straight, but I refuse to focus on his fate. Herein, I will only reveal the necessary portion of his role in this tale to guide you through that which you need to know.

I will refer to this tall, slender seadog, who was more than a decade older than me, as Plan B. He is dubbed this pirate name because he came in at that point on the remodeling project. And, it truly suits him.

Plan B was a handsome, intelligent man who meshed well with people from all backgrounds. As an extrovert and natural storyteller, he was easy to be around and could charm the crown from a queen.

Admittedly, I was attracted to him when we first met, but he was married. However, because we enjoyed talking to each other, we maintained a lighthearted, amicable relationship whenever business brought us together.

Aside from his natural good looks, I was most attracted to his fantastic sense of humor. Sarcastic, witty, and even dry at times, the two of us would be tied up in laughter shortly into any conversation when given the chance.

While working with him on the house, I discovered that we shared many interests. Travel, music, DIY projects, crafts and hobbies, all served as common topics for conversation. We seemed to have the ability to flow together easily, with everything proving effortless between us.

When he asked me out, I wanted to say yes. I thought we paired well and might make the perfect team. However, being aware of his marriage, I felt compelled to address his divorce. Even though it appeared she was no longer active in his life, I needed to make sure, if we were going to date.

"You know I have fun with you and it hasn't occurred to me before, but now I have to ask. Are you divorced?"

"It's been over for years," he said as he nodded and sighed. "She's lived in another state now for several years."

I felt the energy become tense as we approached my car.

"I'm sorry," I said, smiling to ease the tension as I unlocked the car door. "But I had to ask, since you're asking me out."

He quickly opened the door and we stepped aside to let the heat out. His dark-blue eyes were pensive while he studied me, his hands shoved into the front pockets of his cargo shorts.

"I guess that makes sense. So, will you have dinner with me? We can also celebrate the sale of the house," he said with a flirtatious grin.

"Hmm...I think you're onto something," I said with a wink as I slid into the driver's seat. "Call me later to make it a date."

We went to dinner that weekend. It was a leisurely evening filled with conversation and laughter, sprinkled with flirtation. We ended the night on a romantic note by going for a walk on the beach, topped off with a deliciously sultry kiss. It was perfect.

After that night, we moved straight into dating. It was easy being with him and although we spent a lot of time together, neither one of us seemed to be in a hurry for things to progress.

We took frequent bike rides, went to concerts or to the beach to watch the sun set, and did other fun activities together. We could stay in and relax or go out on the town and be perfectly content.

However, after dating a few months, I noticed he seldom introduced me when he saw people he knew. And, if he did, I was always a friend (never a girlfriend), and I wanted to know why.

Was he ashamed of me? Was he keeping his options open? Had he dated that person? I could only speculate, but my instinct told me to pay close attention. I knew if it remained a habit, I would have to inquire.

The next time we were at the grocery store, a woman approached him to say hello. After their brief conversation, during which she looked at me but neither of us were introduced, I knew it was time to bring it up.

"What's that about?" I asked when she was gone.

"What's what about?" he asked, inspecting a bag of pasta.

"Whenever you see people you know, especially women, you rarely introduce me. If you do, I'm only a friend, never your girlfriend. Why?"

"Well, you are my friend. What do you expect?" he asked, tossing the pasta into the cart.

"You do everything with your friends that you do with me? That's interesting," I said, laughing a slight, sarcastic laugh.

"Don't be silly. Of course not, but you are my friend. How I introduce you is my business. I don't need everyone prying into my personal life," he said, shoving the cart ahead. It was clear I had provoked him and he was irritated. After that, he retreated into silence, ending the discussion.

I resented his dismissal and it made me wonder how he saw me fitting into his life. Sure, his personal life was his, but I thought he would be pleased to acknowledge our status, rather than hide it. Based on his response and attitude, I believed he did it to keep his options open.

Rather than turn it into something bigger than necessary, I chose to let it go. Everything else was great between us and I wanted to see how things would evolve naturally, without causing unnecessary drama.

We continued on, spending most evenings and weekends together while maintaining our separate living quarters. This arrangement suited me well as I welcomed the slower pace and having my own space.

Several months into our relationship, his bleach-blond friend, Ingrid, stopped by while we were preparing his home for a hurricane. I met her previously at the investment property, when she stopped in to check it out. Apparently, she sold real estate and had asked to see it.

She looked fantastic in heels and a classy, burgundy dress. I, on the other hand, was covered with filth and downright disgusting from toiling in the heat and grime all day.

She barely acknowledged me while pacing the remaining open space inside the garage. Her legs brushed against each other with every irritated step, her nylons making a disturbing swish-swish sound as she busily avoided obstacles. Her head was twitching as she faced my general direction. Refusing to make eye contact, she asked where she could find Plan B.

"He should be around back," I said.

"Good. I need to speak to him. This place is a mess!" she said with a sneer and a flick of her perfectly manicured hand.

After her observation, she promptly turned on her spiky heel and marched out of the garage on a mission. I moved to a window facing the rear of the house to see what she would do, curiosity getting the best of me.

She hobbled around in the backyard, sinking into the lawn in her high heels. Refusing to take them off, she looked silly all dressed up and fumbling around. I enjoyed watching her struggle, probably a little too much.

When she found him, she had a brief, heated exchange, and then left. After her haughty departure, I too, wanted to talk to him. He was hanging shutters over a bedroom window when I approached.

"Please refresh my mind and tell me again. What exactly is your relationship with her?"

"I already told you. We're just friends," he replied curtly, without looking at me.

"And that's the same title you give me, but we aren't just friends. So, if you two *are* just friends, then why is she so nasty to me?"

"Kendyl, stop exaggerating. She has never said anything negative about you. You need to get over it and accept that I have friends who are women!" he said, his face flushing when he turned to look at me.

"Yes, I know," I replied with a tone of my own. "But, as a friend, I don't treat her with hostility like she does me, whether you witness it or not. So, I must ask, is she aware the two of you are *just* friends?"

The question hung out there, suspended in midair without direction for several tense seconds. He stared at me while wiping the sweat from his brow. When he responded, it was with heightened irritation.

"This is absurd," he said, appearing exasperated. "I'm sure that, as my friend, she's just being overly protective of me." Then he turned abruptly, grabbed the ladder and walked away, ending the discussion.

Once again, I noticed how he managed to circumvent any direct inquiry pertaining to the women in his life and their status, including me. Realizing something was definitely amiss, I remained determined to uncover the truth. However, for the moment, I had more important issues to tend to.

I left him with his attitude and returned home to prepare my place for the approaching storm. After placing the shutters and clearing the patio, I ate lunch, took a hot bath, and then relaxed for a while.

In the late afternoon, I prepared to leave. I washed the dishes, flipped the hot water off and tidied up the living room. After stalling for as long as possible, I packed a few necessities in my bag, put my kitty, Goose, into his carrier, and loaded the car. I took one last look around the place, grabbed Goose's carrier, locked the house, and headed back to Plan B's.

Despite his disposition, we would stay with him for the duration of the storm and its aftermath. Even if he was unpleasant, it was the most sensible course of action. If we lost power for any length of time, we would be more comfortable at his place because I had neither a generator nor a grill, and he had both.

As expected, Plan B was still foul when we arrived. Therefore, I refused to give him the satisfaction of my company until his mood improved.

I unpacked the car and moved Goose into his temporary quarters, choosing to spend my evening with him in solitude. Even if he was unhappy being removed from his home, at least *he* was not sulking. The following day, Plan B lightened up.

A few days later, the hurricane passed and wiped out the electricity, leaving us with plenty of time together, undisturbed. On the second day, I asked about Ingrid again because something was off, and I needed answers. It took several attempts while he evaded questions, but in the end, he admitted they had dated. He insisted it was over but she had not accepted it.

I knew he spent time with her while working on the house several months ago. He never hid it and even invited me to join them for dinner one night at his place. Everything appeared platonic between them and at the time, the depth of their relationship was irrelevant to me.

But now with the truth acknowledged and our new relationship, their status became relevant. And, considering her reaction to my presence, I was not convinced they were over. Therefore, Plan B's reluctant, flippant response was insufficient, and I chose to persist.

When it was all grudgingly disclosed, he revealed they dated for four years and technically, it was not over. Sadly, I realized he had lied and that I was too trusting, once again.

Stop me right here if you must chastise me; I know I have probably earned it. In my defense, which might be pretty weak by now, I am much better at seeing the signs when my emotions are not involved.

But when they are, I am a fully invested partner. And yes, I have been derailed countless times by giving people the benefit of the doubt while trusting them to be honest and true. This relationship was no exception.

I mulled over the new information for a couple of days. I realized I had fallen in love with this man, which skewed my logic. Before consulting myself first and truthfully, last, I made the error of giving *him* the opportunity to choose which one of us he wanted to continue dating.

This, my dear reader, is a mistake I made and you do not have to.

Do yourself a favor. If a similar situation presents itself to you, do not do as I have, by handing them the keys to your treasure. Instead, make the decision for yourself (and for them), by taking charge of your life and cutting them loose.

I urge you to move on and remain available for honest, loving, and true partners who will treat you kindly and with respect. If you do not, they will continue to treat you with disrespect, as my tale shall reveal because, as you probably suspect, I did not cut him loose.

He ended the relationship with her.

I was skeptical yet hopeful, and promised myself that if I were to stay with him, then I would give him a fair second chance.

Chapter 36

'Tis the Season

Hurricane season eventually passed. The holidays were rapidly approaching, when Plan B's employer announced their holiday party. We were lounging in his living room and enjoying the quiet of the afternoon, when he mentioned the event.

"I received an invitation for our company party. Would you like to go with me?" he asked, putting his magazine on the table.

"Of course, I'd love to. When is it?"

"It's December 7th," he said, sporting a mischievous grin.

"What's the grin for? What aren't you telling me?" I asked, sliding onto his lap.

"How do you feel about going to New York in the winter?" he asked, wrapping his arms around me.

"Oh, that'll be awesome! When do we leave?" I asked, jumping up, only to have him pull me back down.

"I'll work on the details and let you know. I can't wait to introduce you to everyone. They've all heard so much about you," he said, sealing the deal with a passionate kiss.

We discussed the event while fixing dinner and again before saying goodnight. I was excited about the party and looked forward to making plans for the trip. We always had fun on our weekend getaways, and I was confident this one would be the best.

Thrilled with the invitation, but not having a winter wardrobe readily available, it was time to go shopping. I went to my favorite winter specialty shop in Fort Lauderdale and found a chic cashmere sweater and a beautiful pair of soft, classy corduroys, all in winter white.

My current clothing selection held an elegant, skin-hugging, black silk sweater that looked amazing with either the corduroys or a pair of jeans. Envisioning the collection, it was stunning with my long, black coat and the black mink earmuffs I borrowed from Brooke.

For the main event, I planned on wearing a deep-red, silk blouse with black silk pants that belonged to a gorgeous two-piece outfit Money Man had contributed. The pants were whisper soft with wide legs and when I stood still, they looked like a floor-length skirt. The outfit would be striking yet understated and make the perfect final piece for the weekend.

In the meantime, we discussed the travel arrangements. Plan B would leave at the beginning of the week and I would follow later for the weekend festivities. In the end, we decided I should arrive the afternoon of the party.

"I prefer the flight arriving at two," I said. "That way, I'll have time to relax and have a bite to eat before the party."

"That may be, but I have to work and can't pick you up until after five. I think you'll have to take the later flight that gets in at five thirty. That'll work because cocktails are at six and dinner is at seven, so you'll still have time to get ready."

"Do you really think they're going to make everyone work until close, when cocktails are at six? And do you think they'd mind if you left to pick me up, if so? You work from a satellite office in the first place," I said, finding his logic irrational.

"I don't know Kendyl, but this is what I want to do and the decision's been made. I don't want to have to worry about it either way."

"Okay, then please have something for me to eat when I arrive. In fact, please bring it with you to the airport. You know I have low blood sugar and they won't let me take food on the plane."

"I'll make sure there's plenty to snack on," he said, smiling to soften the mood set by his previous tone.

The tickets were purchased and the days zipped by at a delightfully rapid pace. We were both excited to visit New York in the winter, with the added anticipation of a great event and our first holiday party together.

My departure date arrived and the rain came with it. As the hours ticked by, the severity of the weather increased, causing localized flooding. Anticipating traffic delays, I decided to leave early for the airport.

Wearing five-inch mules, I ran through the rain to the car. I loaded the bags, slid in behind the wheel, and started it up. En route to the airport, the rain became torrential and visibility was low, slowing traffic to a crawl.

Even though I left early, I was anxious about the weather, hoping to make my flight. The typical twenty-minute drive took well over an hour, and by the time I found the long-term parking, I was coming unhinged.

My nerves were frazzled when I stepped out of the car in my leather mules, now firmly planted in an inch of water. I waded over to the passenger side to gather my bags and as I came around, I saw the shuttle bus approaching my stop.

I rushed to grab my garment bag and carry-on, which was a simple paper shopping bag. When I pulled them from the car, the bag's bottom broke and its contents plummeted into the pool of rainwater below, scattering at my feet.

My frustration gathering steam faster than a rabbit being chased by a hungry fox, I scratched frantically at the bobbing items, scooping them into the bag and folding it over to keep the contents secure. Clutching the paper bag with one hand, I tossed the garment bag over my shoulder and ran for the shuttle.

Drenched from head to toe, I scrambled onto the bus and fell into the first open seat. Peeling the soaked, silk sweater away from my skin, I silently cursed the heavy jeans, now strangling my legs like compression socks that were a size too small.

While I struggled, the shuttle made its way through a full tour of the airport's grounds and eventually arrived at the terminal. I bolted from the bus, still needing to check in for my flight. Running inside, I found the line and patiently waited behind several other weather-weary travelers.

I felt like I needed to lighten my load after the morning's events, and opted to check my garment bag with the agent. I was on a direct flight and confident the airline would not lose it between here and there.

I removed my camera and surrendered my luggage with a sigh of relief. I then proceeded to the bookstore to replace my torn, dilapidated shopping bag. Armed with a new one, I transferred the items and shook off the day before dashing for the gate.

We boarded immediately and as I took my seat, I began to relax. Taking several long, deep breaths, I sank back and closed my eyes. Thankfully, I made my flight; the rest was up to the pilot.

We waited on the tarmac, our departure delayed by the persistent, torrential downpour. Forty-five minutes later, we were cleared for takeoff.

When the wheels left the ground, I looked at my watch. I realized then how the earlier flight would have provided a stress-free arrival, while avoiding the series of recent inconveniences.

I cleared my thoughts because that flight was irrelevant. I wanted to have a great time and refused to let anything ruin my weekend. Exhausted, I attempted a nap to recharge for the evening's event.

The flight was two hours and went by quickly. We arrived at the gate thirty minutes later than scheduled, rolling in at six o'clock and right at the top of the party's cocktail hour. I was relieved the day was over and looked forward to a hot bath, followed by a great evening.

Plan B was waiting at the gate and greeted me with a hug and a kiss. I sighed, allowing the peaceful moment to linger.

"I'm glad you made it. Why was your plane so late?" he asked, taking the shopping bag and grabbing my hand.

"The weather was terrible in Florida. I'll tell you about my day once and then I'd love to forget it. I checked my bag, so we need to pick it up."

On the way to retrieve my luggage, I recounted the morning's events and asked if he had my snack. Admitting he forgot it, he then proceeded to gloat about his day. As predicted, the company had closed at noon, providing him the opportunity to enjoy the afternoon like a tourist. Perfect for him, I thought. Too bad he did not book the earlier flight.

We arrived at baggage claim and waited for my garment bag. Everyone from my flight came and went, revealing an empty carousel. I was looking around for help, when a scowling woman approached us.

"Are you Ms. Jameson?" she asked.

"Yes?"

"Come with me. You must confirm a few things about your luggage," she said, walking briskly toward a service entrance.

Plan B and I exchanged questioning glances as we followed behind. Meanwhile, my blood sugar was plummeting, zapping my energy as it fell. When we entered the back room, I stopped short.

There was a long banquet table against the wall with my belongings strung out across the surface. My garment bag was torn apart, resting at the other end of the table. Ripped open and nearly shredded in some places, it appeared as though my clothes had been heaved from its bowels.

The woman snatched up her clipboard and requested the baggage claim ticket with an air of impatience, her hand outstretched and waiting. I found the ticket and handed it over, trying to process the jumble before me. She started making notes and tapping her pen against the clipboard while I silently stared at the shredded items.

"We need to take inventory of your clothes. As you can see, we've had a little problem," she said.

I was mesmerized by the mess, stuck in a state of disbelief. I barely heard her speaking and it took a moment before I realized what she said. Holding up a sleeve that had been ripped from its blouse, I showed it to her. The frayed red threads dangled freely where there used to be a seam.

"Little? You call this little? This was all I brought for the weekend," I said slowly, inspecting the remnants of my wardrobe. Selecting the grease-smeared corduroys and sweater, I held them up next for closer examination. Items new and perfect a few hours ago were now ruined and worthless.

The room was still while I assessed the damage. "I packed all of my clothes in here, except for what I'm wearing. Do you see their condition? This is not little," I said quietly, methodically picking through the heap in slow motion. "What happened? Why is everything torn apart and marked with a thick, black grease?"

"The bag got caught on one of the wheels of the conveyor belt and was torn in half," she replied flatly while glancing at her notepad. She watched me for several seconds and then sighed. "Look," she said, waving her clipboard over the heap of fabric, "you have to tell me how much this all cost right now. And, before we pay you anything, you'll have to show receipts for proof. So, let's get on with it."

"Are you serious? Some things I have receipts for, while others I don't. They weren't all bought yesterday. And these," I said, picking up the broken mink earmuffs and holding on to them, "aren't even mine. They belong to a friend who was kind enough to lend them to me. You'll have to work with what I can give you. After all, I'm the one compromised by this *little* problem. Not you, and not your airline," I said, sifting through the rest of the pile.

"You'll have to put those back on the table," she demanded, pointing to the earmuffs with her pen. "Everything we're paying for stays here for our records."

"No. I'll be taking these with me and whatever else I can salvage. I have to prove to her that I'm not stealing her earmuffs," I said, moving on to the silk pants. "And this pair of pants, now scarred, is the only thing I might be able to wear this weekend because both pant legs are still attached. So, they're going too," I said, draping them over my arm.

I didn't care what her rules were. She was rigid and lacked empathy. In addition, her nasty attitude was making the situation worse, and I was rapidly losing the minuscule shred of patience I had left.

I was pacing to maintain a level of calm, but my sugar level was too depleted and I started to shake. I looked around and found Plan B tucked deep into a corner in the background, making sure he would not be called upon to help with this awful woman.

"Will you please get me something to eat? I'm getting a headache and need something fast," I said quietly. He looked at me as though I had twelve heads. "Are you seriously giving me that look?" I asked through gritted teeth, keeping my voice low. "Do you remember when I asked you to bring a snack to the airport? Please do *not* act like I'm out of line and just do it. In case you haven't noticed, I'm dealing with an issue."

Sighing and turning back to her, I heard him ask another employee where he could find a snack. Eventually, he returned with a small juice and resumed his role as a helpless but intrigued spectator.

The entire process lasted thirty minutes. Once complete, we left with my replacement tote in tow, carrying the few things I could salvage.

Arriving at the hotel, I told Plan B that I was going to take a bath to decompress before going to the party. We took the elevator to our floor, and as we entered the room, I asked again about the snacks.

"We're going to be late for dinner if you do that! What snacks are you talking about? I don't have any," he said, throwing his jacket on the bed and casting a glare my way.

How dare he give me an attitude or even an ounce of grief after the afternoon I had, I thought. Refusing to give him the fight it appeared he was seeking, I practiced restraint and kept my voice low.

"Um, let me think," I said, returning his glare. "Oh yeah. The snacks you promised to bring to the airport. The same ones we discussed when you insisted I take the later flight. Oh, and about that. I asked for the earlier flight so I could chill before the party. Now, I'm going to relax and then I'll get ready. In the meantime, and I hope this isn't too much of an inconvenience for you, will you *please* get me something to eat?"

I kicked off my mules and threw the tote on the bed. Turning my back to him in defiance, I went into the bathroom and started the bath.

He huffed as he left and returned a few minutes later with free cookies from the lobby. He tossed them onto the bureau and said they would have to suffice until dinner, shamelessly aggravated with me for making us late.

I snatched up the cookies and retreated to the bathroom. Sinking into the tub of hot water, I tuned out the day, promising myself that fifteen minutes of pure bliss would carry me through.

Savoring the delicious chocolate chip cookies, I wondered fleetingly how a grown man could be completely useless.

Chapter 37

Me Beauty and Me Lies

Refreshed from the bath, I dressed for the party from my limited options. I pulled the black silk sweater back on and slid into the stunning, black silk pants and mules. I brushed my hair smooth until it resembled a shining sheet of silk that added perfect contrast to the all-black ensemble.

Completing the look, I applied mascara, eye shadows in warm, natural tones, and a touch of red lipstick. The make-up brightened my appearance after the long day. Looking in the mirror, I was pleased with the result and knew I had maximized on my available resources. It was time to leave.

Upon our tardy arrival, we learned dinner would be served later than scheduled. Pleased to have a few minutes to mingle, Plan B put on his cloak of charm and began greeting his co-workers. Having a few witnesses around, he asked sweetly if I wanted a drink.

"How sweet! Thank you, honey, but I'll get it. You stay and visit."

"Okay, I'll be over there," he said, pointing to another group of peers.

I knew he wanted to make himself look good to the ladies and welcomed the opportunity to create space between us. I strolled over to the bar and perused the finger foods, made my selections, and ordered a drink.

A few minutes later, I was armed with a cocktail and a few snacks to calm my nerves. Officially prepared for the evening to kick off, I joined Plan B. He introduced me (as his girlfriend) to his colleagues who were visibly surprised at our considerable age difference.

It was interesting that when in New York and removed from his local social circle, I was referred to as his girlfriend. I suppose acknowledging our status at the party was less threatening to his personal life, because this crowd lived far from South Florida. The age difference between us also made him look like a sexy stud, and he was clearly eating up the attention with every comment and approving raise of the eyebrows.

Loving the spotlight, Plan B decided to entertain a group of ladies with my day's events. I was happy to let him have it. My day had been long enough and I was quietly enjoying the buzz in the room with my Appletini. I was sipping along when I tuned in to what he was saying.

"You wouldn't believe it. She took us to the back room, and there was Kendyl's bag, ripped in half. It was a mess! She took one look at her clothes and started screaming. I had to calm her down and remind her they were just clothes and could be replaced," he said, watching me closely.

Gasps escaped from several members of his female audience and his expression revealed he was enjoying the whole scene. They were enthralled with his version of my experience, and I understood why.

His embellishments added a level of excitement to my drama, but unfortunately, the wrong kind for me to accept. A few exaggerations were one thing, but a blatant misrepresentation of my behavior was different.

However, this was a game to him and I knew it. I decided he'd had enough fun at my expense, and it was time to set the story straight.

"If you're telling my story, you should relay it the way it happened since I'm standing right here," I said, maintaining an even tone. "I never raised my voice. Not to her, and not to you. Nor did I lose my temper. Please show me a little respect for how gracefully I *did* handle it, especially under the circumstances."

"Oh my gosh! I would've lost it!" a woman exclaimed. "I would've been crying, and screaming, and throwing a fit!"

"Me too!" said another ardent listener. "I wouldn't have come to the party tonight! I can't believe you're here. You're so calm and you look like a million bucks. I love your pants!" she said, lightly touching my forearm and visually scanning my outfit.

She turned her attention to Plan B. "Well, you *are* going to take her shopping and buy her clothes this weekend, aren't you?" she asked. There was a twinkle in her eye as she nudged my arm with her elbow.

I laughed at the question and the involuntary, horrified expression he quickly replaced with a smile. "I highly doubt that'll happen, but thanks for trying," I said, nodding in her direction.

He was obviously uncomfortable with the pickle he was in, and shot me a warning look. I returned the unspoken message with a sweet, knowing smile. I understood how tight he was when it came to spending money on me and knew he dreaded being exposed to his adoring fans.

Sadly, he was unwilling to part with his cash unless he was guaranteed a direct and immediate reward. He would not receive any pleasure from buying clothes for me and therefore, it would not be on the agenda.

While I thought it over, the ladies continued discussing how they would have responded to the clothing catastrophe until we were ushered in for dinner. As we were seated, I too, wore my cloak of charm, determined to be a gracious guest. Everything proceeded without a hitch, and by the end of the event, we had convinced the crowd we were a happy couple.

The rest of the weekend went surprisingly well. We savored amazing meals at upscale restaurants and mingled with his peers. We went shopping and I found an identical pair of mink earmuffs to replace Brooke's, and purchased them myself. Even though Plan B was scarce at checkout, I was pleased to have resolved the issue.

As long as I pretended Friday's events never happened and asked for nothing, Plan B was happy and we had a good time. With the weekend behind us, things seemed to settle down when we returned to Florida where he no longer had a rapt audience.

In hindsight, I should have recognized the weekend's events as a red flag and ended the relationship after our trip. But I did not, apparently having more to learn and subconsciously choosing to continue.

I cannot tell you if I stayed because I was too involved with other priorities in my life to notice, or if I had become complacent. Either way, I did nothing, and can only assume I was comforted in having someone to be with, regardless of how he treated me.

Several smooth, enjoyable months passed, and I believed my previous thoughts of being in love with him were valid, despite the signs I chose to ignore. Therefore, being true to myself and my emotions, I told him how I felt one evening at my place after dinner.

He sat motionless, offering silence as his response. Surprised by his absence in the moment, I was utterly perplexed. I honestly didn't see that coming because he claimed to be crazy about me.

However, not one to push an issue, I let it lie. After all, I want someone to reciprocate if they mean it, not to appease me. If he wasn't ready or did not love me, then I could accept it, even if it did sting a bit.

After his lingering silence, which was broken only when I changed the topic, I knew I had to re-evaluate our relationship. I realized something nondescript loomed between us and blamed it, whatever it was, for why we could not move forward as a couple.

I examined our relationship over the following days. I forced myself to be honest and acknowledge the details not lining up. Although I could not pinpoint what it was, there were too many particulars nagging at me and they all appeared to be pointing to the same thing.

The black hole between us that he pretended did not exist, was growing larger and I had to solve the mystery. Considering his ample talent at evading topics of depth and value, I knew better than to address it with him without a few facts. Whatever it was, it remained an anomaly for the time being.

Summer came and went without a notable incident or any change in our status. Labor Day arrived, and we spent the morning at his house washing our cars before going to his friends' place for a barbecue. I was soaping up my sporty GT when he came over to volunteer instruction.

"You're doing that wrong," he said, pointing at my car's sudsy top.

"Really? I've washed my car for years and it always looks great."

"Well, maybe to *you*. But you never start with the top. Wash the wheels first, discard the water, and then with new water, work from the top down."

"Uh huh. But, I have a convertible. So, I do the top, then the wheels and discard the water. With fresh water, I wash from the top down. You do realize that there's more than one way to wash a car, don't you?" I asked, rinsing the top off and moving to the tires.

"Maybe so, but my way is better," he said, returning to his own set of wheels.

"I don't see how your way is any better. I think you're just looking for something to correct me on again," I said, rubbing out my frustration on a wheel. After this conversation, it would probably be cleaner than ever.

Focusing on my chore, I reflected on his disapproving comments about how I did things, and yet he never offered to do them for me. I couldn't tell if he was trying to start a fight or being parental, but neither worked for me.

The previous few days had been peppered with similar judgments. He claimed I poached eggs incorrectly (they were perfect), a fork was not to be used as a whisk, and a butter knife was *never* to be used as a screwdriver. Apparently, he at least approved of me washing my car with water.

Naturally, we finished the cars in silence and afterward, I went home to shower and dress for dinner. When he arrived at my place, he seemed a little sore from the earlier dispute. I was over it, but he had a tendency to sulk and wallow a while to keep the mood going. As usual, the drive was quiet and the air between us was stiff.

When we arrived at the party, his mood shifted and he was instantly jovial toward everyone else. We greeted the hostess and were assigned to setting the table while other tasks were completed by other guests. We gathered the settings and went to work.

"The napkins don't go there," he whispered across the table.

"Where would you like them to go, Plan B, if folded neatly under the silverware isn't correct?" I asked sweetly, without looking at him.

"You're doing it wrong! I can't believe you don't know how to set a table!" he whispered loudly.

Without answering my question and immediately following his retort, he turned abruptly and strolled into the kitchen, shifting gears once again. Smiling and jostling with the hostess, he carried on, occasionally glancing over to see if I was paying attention.

He was looking for a reaction he did not receive. Whenever his efforts to irritate me were unsuccessful, he used this tactic to try to elicit a negative response. Apparently, he needed to soothe his bruised ego by pushing me into doing something wherein I would inadvertently make myself look like a fool in front of others.

Recognizing his pattern, I ignored him and enjoyed the festivities. Dinner came and went and everyone magically found their napkins. When the evening was over, he resumed his silent treatment and took me home.

We parted on a chilly note that previously would have left me scratching my head, asking myself what I did wrong and wondering how I could fix it. But now that I understood his behavioral pattern, I remained unaffected by his attitude. I was truly happy to be home alone in my own space, knowing his mood would linger until he chose to give it up.

He would be dreadful to be around for several days, and then snap out of it. He was practiced at delivering silent treatments to make me wonder what I did to upset him. However, when asked, he never had an answer.

Dating him was like being on a roller coaster, with his moods quickly going up and down and his attitude twisting and turning abruptly without warning. We had seamless fun together and when everything was ideal, he would create a problem. It was as though he could handle only so much peace and happiness before he had to disrupt everything.

Why would I think this behavior was abnormal? My father and most of the men I dated had behaved similarly.

I could not recall a time when I did not have to tolerate and adjust to others' abrupt mood changes to keep the peace. It was also normal for me to have to wait and see what their mood was before deciding how to proceed. Unfortunately, I was accustomed to smothering my enthusiasm, personality and sense of humor while hoping for a harmonious outcome.

Additionally, I believed I was in love with Plan B, and could not walk away because of this up-and-down pattern. The consistent inconsistency in our relationship gave pause to wonder, but with my emotions in play and without a better example to follow, I persisted.

After he came around from the last silent treatment, things smoothed out again for a while. It was closing in on his birthday, when I surprised him with tickets to the theatre and a night out. I had invested time, thought, and money into making his birthday event fun and memorable and was excited with how everything was coming together.

After buying the tickets, I focused on what to wear and thought about how he always urged me to wear more red. He said I would look amazing and asked me to consider it. Bending to his pleas, I decided to wear a new red dress for our special evening.

As a fair blonde, the best shade for me is a blue-based red. Although it can be difficult to find, I was determined. I shopped relentlessly for the perfect dress and eventually found one. I bought it, the shoes, and the handbag to complement.

It was a sensational satin cocktail dress with thin straps, a sweetheart neckline, and fitted bodice. Delicate ruby-red lace enhanced the neckline, adding a touch of subtle elegance. The skirt was double layered, flaring at the hips and continuing to mid-calf. The dress was classy and elegant, with plenty of sex appeal despite the lack of skin showing.

The night arrived, and I donned my new dress with anticipation of how much he would love it. I curled my hair and applied minimal make-up to complete the look. I slipped my feet into the new black stilettos, admiring the intricate red inlay on the toes. They were stunning and the perfect accessory to the dress.

I stepped in front of the full-length mirror and scanned my reflection, front and back. I had succeeded with my goal and felt unstoppable. When he knocked on the door, I opened it with a sultry smile and a slow, scintillating twirl to kick off the evening.

However, my enthusiasm vanished like mist into fog when I finished my twirl and saw his face. It was void of expression, resembling a blank sheet of paper, lacking even the slightest hint of emotion or sign of life. Still, I ventured on.

"Do you like it?" I asked with a sexy smile, fanning the skirt out with my hands.

"It would've looked better in black. Let's go," he said, marching ahead to open the car door. Hurt and disappointed, I trailed behind like a balloon losing its air, slowly descending to its ruin.

What a jerk. We had dated long enough for him to know the dress was new and the red was for him. Yet for some reason, he felt the need to crush me with a single blow.

I picked myself up a few minutes into the ride, determined to have a great time regardless of his crappy attitude. I knew I had not provoked him and his mood was not my fault. Whatever his problem was, it was all his.

Inside the theatre, I realized what at least part of his problem was. Everyone (okay, it *felt* like everyone) noticed me, and many did a double take. Several people smiled and even complimented me.

Their words of approval confirmed I wore the dress well, despite Plan B's lack of charm. In fact, his one, worthless statement was the only comment he offered about my appearance, and he didn't have much to say about the event, either. In truth, it was a quiet evening all around.

When the night came to a close, he took me home in silence. I was relieved when we arrived and once again, pleased to be alone in my peaceful environment, which should have been a sign in and of itself.

The evening spurred an internal reaction, leading me to reflect on recent comments, remarks, and events. I noticed how he consistently created opportunities to squash me, while working to undermine my self-esteem.

His condescending clips and degrading comments were becoming more frequent. He appeared to take pleasure in selecting the best time to belittle me discreetly in front of others. His passive-aggressive approach forced me to either defend myself and look like an idiot, or smile and carry on, such as when we were at dinner on Labor Day.

After several incidents when my intuition was heightened and my eyes were opened, I slowly withdrew emotionally. Finally, I started looking at us from a different perspective.

I wanted to wrap my head around what was going on with the relationship, which clearly only I was invested in. Even though this involved more time, I required certainty to avoid regret.

Therefore, comfortable with waiting to see how things would unfold, I sat back to observe him in action. I allowed him to do whatever he wanted, treating me however he saw fit. I no longer questioned him on anything.

He became complacent, possibly assuming I had submitted and accepted his rules. Instead, I was quietly monitoring everything between us.

In the meantime, I decided to do something out of character, and conducted a bit of background research on him. Nothing extreme or crazy, mind you, only easily accessible public information.

As I collected my data, my suspicion was confirmed and everything started to make sense. The black hole between us was becoming bigger and more ominous, and I was amazed (and disappointed) at my naïveté.

The reason he always became defensive and abrupt whenever I dared to discuss our relationship or my role in his life, would soon be exposed. The final piece required to prove my theory would be the answer to the question I was determined to ask him in person.

I called him at work the afternoon of my discovery and asked to see him later at his place. He agreed to meet after a few minutes of questioning me, sensing something was brewing when I refused an explanation.

I arrived that evening as promised and on a mission. Now indifferent, I was numb to his mood. I had one question for him to answer, and hopefully this time he would be truthful.

I walked in and found him in the kitchen, preparing dinner. I waited until he looked up to acknowledge me, demanding direct eye contact for my inquiry.

"Are you divorced?"

Chapter 38

Walk the Plank

The question hovered for several moments with weighted silence like an executioner's axe, right before it drops. And then he erupted.

"What are you doing looking into my background?" he yelled, slamming a cast-iron frying pan onto the counter. His face darkened as he shook with anger. "Who are you to violate *my* privacy? And where do you get off sneaking around behind my back?" he shouted, consumed with rage.

"*Your* privacy?" I shouted back. "You've been lying to me this entire time, and you want to talk about privacy? You forfeited it when you started dating me under the pretense of being a single, divorced man. Not to mention, you were also dating Ingrid! If you were honest, none—"

"Kendyl! When are you going to realize that *everything is not about you?*"

"How is this *not* about me?"

Avoiding my questions as usual, he launched into yelling accusations, claiming I was to blame for our relationship issues. Disregarding that two people cannot move forward in a relationship while one of them is not only lying, but also still married to someone else, he forged on.

Holding nothing back, he blamed me for things of which I was unaware and uninvolved. He caused such a ruckus you would have sworn someone had been shot, sliced into pieces, and served to him for his dinner.

Yet, none of it was mine and I knew it.

I was neither the cause of, nor the cure for, his issues. Once again, I knew they were all his. Shaking my head, I turned and quietly left while he continued yelling, his venomous words chasing me to the door.

I slid into the driver's seat of my beautiful convertible, relieved to have the confrontation behind me. The roar of the V8 engine tuned him out when I fired it up, creating a powerful statement that carried me home and away from his absurdity.

Sadly, it took me way too long to sort the details, but shame on him for being deceitful. Even though he was not divorced, she lived in a different state. In his mind, that made it acceptable to dismiss his marriage.

This singular, seemingly harmless detail, along with everything it represented, was the first issue standing in the way of our relationship moving forward. Setting aside his marriage, the other truth remained that he had lied and it was a serious deception.

Blaming me repeatedly for the turmoil in our relationship only strengthened my desire to ascertain the root of the problem. Obviously, he did not expect me to discover his truth and call him out on it. But I knew I was not to blame, and upon my discovery, his method was revealed.

Using lies as tools, he created an avalanche of problems starting with one issue, which led to one problem after another. Implementing lies to hide other deceptions, he also used them to bury his emotions. His strategy allowed him to deny his realities, which then became the shadows in mine.

After working it all out, I realized the depth of his deception and knew I had to make a decision. However, after his reluctant and long-overdue acknowledgment of his marital status, I did not walk away immediately.

I continued on for two weeks, keeping a distinct distance between us. The latest revelation had occurred quickly, and I needed to extricate myself from the relationship a bit more before ending it.

Moving forward without expectations, the following weeks revealed more lies, and the facts were overwhelming. I realized if everything I discovered did not force me to question my self-respect, then nothing would make me face my truth.

When I drew our relationship to a close and it was time for him to walk the plank, he resisted. He promised he would not lie again if I gave him another chance. I refused his request. I knew he didn't love me and it was another lie to get what he wanted.

A month later, he filed for divorce and completed the process. When he told me, he said he thought that was all I wanted and it should fix everything. He also said he loved me, as if it should matter anymore.

When the news of the divorce and his proclamation of love did not sway me, he continued his pursuit. He pushed forward for three more years, relentlessly requesting another chance and claiming he would treat me right.

But I remembered the deceit, condescending comments, unnecessary fights, snide remarks, silent treatments, manipulations, and variations of everything somehow always being my fault. I knew he would revert to his old ways when he thought he was safe, and why would I want to go back to that?

Even though he claimed to love me, I questioned his motive because of his manipulative nature. I think he wanted to redeem his ego and if I gave in, then he could be the one to end the relationship. Or maybe it was to avoid loneliness. Regardless of his intent, I am convinced it was never about love.

I doubt he learned anything from our time together, because his behavior was irrational for someone who wanted to remain a part of my life. However, I learned plenty.

With respect to relationships, I learned that red flags are red for a reason. I have never benefited from ignoring them, and despite how many excuses I make for someone, the facts are what they are.

I realized if someone does not treat me with respect from the beginning, then they never will. In addition, if I settle for less than I deserve, I am guaranteed to receive even less than I settled for.

I also saw how competitive he was, and rather than being pleased and proud to be with me, he was always measuring and keeping score. I realized that if I am to be in a relationship, then I need to be with someone who wants to see me shine, not snuff out my flame.

Throughout this relationship, I experienced an excess of manipulation used to keep me in my place. Numerous attempts were made to suppress my fun, positive qualities and instead, erode my self-esteem and infuse self-doubt.

From this pirate, then, I stole back my personality and public image, if you will. I terminated the power struggle over who decided how I would behave and be represented to the masses.

I took back the pieces that make me who I am, and put myself back together again. Through this process, I also restored peace to my daily life by eliminating the unnecessary stress he brought into my world.

In the end, the entire relationship was one massive lesson geared toward understanding myself and what matters to me.

Therefore, I must say thank you, Plan B!

You were one heck of a teacher and truly drove home the point. Although our relationship was overflowing with lessons, there is one that stands out above the rest and I will never forget.

Even though it was not your intention, you reminded me that I am worthy of receiving love and respect, and I must never settle for less. And sadly, as the tale reveals, you did not accomplish this because you treated me with love and respect, but rather because you were incapable of doing either.

So, in essence Plan B, I guess in the end, it *was* all about me.

I like to believe this was my final class on such relationships and hope to never repeat any of these lessons.

Will I pass the next test?

I suppose this is the only question that remains.

Chapter 39

The Gibbet Cage

I have told you a long tale about the pirates of my soul, the men who came into my life and tried to steal my most prized possession to increase their own value. I revealed my weaknesses to you, exposed and hung in the gibbet cage, to discourage you from repeating my experiences and to learn from them instead.

I am neither proud, nor ashamed, of having dated these men. Instead, I reviewed each relationship to analyze it. In doing so, I acknowledged my weaknesses and strengths and discovered the kind of relationship that would benefit me most.

I did not seek professional help for my recovery from the aftermath of any of these relationships. I chose to tackle the residual effects headfirst on my own, starting with the girl in the mirror. By being brutally honest, I was able to take responsibility for what was mine and make necessary improvements.

Understanding the benefits of doing my personal homework, I urge others to embrace the opportunity and do the same for themselves. Study relationships to discover what, if any, lessons are present.

If indeterminable, yet you believe something is amiss, then I suggest being willing to seek guidance. Life is too short to repeat negative experiences, of which, many are entirely avoidable.

If I am writing to *you*, I trust you will persist! Be determined to find out what matters most to you while making your soul sing.

In summation of the relationships and my personal, hard-core review, I share with you here the most important pieces of treasure. These are by which I maintain my stance on how I expect to be treated and what I will not accept in my life from others, regardless of their relationship with me.

I believe in my self-worth and self-respect and know I do not have to settle for less than I deserve, and I refuse to. These reminders keep me on pace. They provide the necessary courage and strength to stand up against any fears others try to impose upon me based on their insecurities, wants or needs.

I share these with you, because I want you to draw from them the same strength and courage. To be able to protect yourself, your self-worth, and self-respect from the seething scoundrels who seek to steal your soul and smother your happiness. I eagerly encourage you to apply them if they fit.

One of the key pieces I took from my stint with Bad Boy was realizing when someone is creating problems, only to be the hero by saving me from them. To me, this is an example of passive-aggressive behavior used to create a codependent relationship, which has the potential to become dangerous on numerous levels.

I understand when someone is a rebel and drifter in life that we will never align for a positive outcome. I realized that regardless of how much potential I think someone has, unless they feel the same, they will never pursue it.

I learned that I must *keep my expectations of others within their limitations.* This allows them to maintain their individuality, while preventing disappointment and frustration for me. It also provides clarity about the type of relationship we have and whether or not it works for me.

Driver was not a completely negative force. He was unable to steal my soul (mainly chiseled away at my self-respect), but he did not embrace it or try to feed it, which left me feeling like I did not matter to him.

He participated in my life in a few ways, while excluding me from his whenever it suited him. His overall lack of interest in me proved to be insightful to where he placed his priorities.

He certainly had his moments when he was arrogant and belittling, but after considering all angles in my review, I hope it was because of his age when we dated. I am grateful I heeded my gut instinct and learned that I need to *listen to and act on my intuition more often.*

As for Money Man, I learned nothing in particular about me because I am not naturally driven by the possession of bright, shiny objects. I do want a man to adore me. If he chooses to shower me with gifts of love and affection, I want such tokens to be genuine and not symbolic of strings attached to a predetermined outcome of some kind of ownership.

I understand how the obsession to possess things or people could suck the life out of someone. I was thrilled to have escaped when I did and learned in reality, *all things that glitter are not gold.*

My experience with Casanova taught me how endings always bring forth new beginnings. I no longer fear change and am much better at embracing endings. I took a giant leap into the unknown when I left him and although it was scary, I knew I had to do it to save myself.

I discovered if I dare to take action and give myself wings, there will always be assistance, if necessary. Should I lose altitude, *I will always receive what I need, to arrive where I am supposed to be going.*

I also learned when someone says they love me, it does not guarantee they mean it or know how to love me the way I need to be loved. And, because of this, I experienced what it meant to be in a relationship and still be lonely.

In addition, I was revived by the incredible power of dictating closure to a situation. By creating my own closure, I reacquired complete control over my soul and used my courage to set myself free, becoming empowered to move forward without regret.

And yes, then there is Mon Homme. In addition to what I learned pertaining to addictions as previously depicted, I realized my fighting spirit will not go quietly and this is good.

I understand I must take care of me (and I will), when my happiness or well-being is at stake. I have given myself permission to walk away without guilt and know it is acceptable to not have all the answers.

I also discovered the importance of recognizing when something or someone is not healthy for me and letting it go, no matter how badly I want it. I accepted the value provided by the release, and no longer fight to hold on to unhealthy attachments. I know now that *when someone's decisions are destroying my life, I must let them go for my survival.*

My encounter with Rebound Man taught me it should not have happened. I had recently ended an intense relationship wherein I was truly in love. I realized that with a weak and wounded heart, I was vulnerable and susceptible to becoming someone's prey.

I learned when a substantial relationship ends, it must be properly mourned. Preventing further injury or heartache requires the appropriate time and space to heal. I also discovered how *it is better to be alone and happy, than in a relationship and miserable.*

My experience with Leech reminded me that I don't need a man to give me the courage or strength to accomplish anything I want in life. I am not inadequate because I am not physically strong enough or educated in a topic. I can hire it out, or teach myself.

I recognize the signs of a con man and a mooch and know I will not take in any more squatters. And most importantly, I learned that once a scoundrel, always a scoundrel, and it *never pays to mix with a scoundrel.*

And, now for Plan B and the lessons I gathered from our convoluted and twisted relationship.

First, I will admit I was forced to revisit how my instincts and intuition are never wrong and exist to protect me, if I pay attention. This particular lesson repeatedly presented itself, and I hope this time I have it down.

With this pirate, I experienced how a relationship built on lies will never succeed. It cannot amount to one of value and longevity, because it is missing a solid foundation. Both parties must be honest for quality to exist and a true, loving relationship to blossom and prevail.

In addition, both individuals must be emotionally available and want the same outcome. It became evident that in our case, we had different ideas and expectations of what we wanted from a relationship.

I also realized once I accepted a certain behavior from him, the manner in which he treated me continued to decline. I know with respect to relationships and how I am treated, it *is* all about me, because I am the one who has to live with the consequences.

And from all pirates collectively, which probably equals an entire ship's crew, I learned I must be careful with my heart and soul. I must set the bar higher and it cannot be negotiated.

I am no longer concerned with whose feelings I might hurt if I confront them about their lies and deceit.

I will not be berated, belittled, neglected, disrespected, emotionally or verbally abused, and pretend it is acceptable even when people are present and it would cause a scene. *It is not acceptable.*

After studying these relationships, I decided if any of this happens, the man in question will not be allowed to try it again. My tolerance for taking abuse in any form from weak, insecure, unstable individuals has been tapped and the barrel is empty.

And then, there is the lesson from life itself.

Quite possibly, what it was trying to teach me all along is that if something is no longer a positive contributor to my life, then it must be discarded. Whether it is a relationship or job I have outgrown, if allowed to persist, it will prevent me from moving forward.

In addition, I have noticed that when I refuse to move forward on my own, life takes over. Without pause or room for negotiation, it creates circumstances which force an ending to inexorably propel me into my future.

And it always does.

Chapter 40

Coming About

Where does a pattern of negative relationships similar to each other stem from? How does it start? How does someone repeatedly subject themselves to unnecessary drama and negativity? Why do they allow themselves to become involved with people who disrespect and abuse them?

If you are a person who finds yourself in a pattern such as mine, then maybe this will bring a speck of hope to you. While I was bouncing along from pirate to pirate, I was blissfully unaware of being locked in a pattern.

Every relationship seemed different, and each man appeared on the surface to be an improvement over the last one. That is, with the exception of the two who immediately followed the disheartening breakup with Mon Homme. However, the underlying theme cannot be denied.

But once it has been acknowledged and identified, it can be addressed.

Many people find themselves repeating their relationship types with only the names and faces changing in between. Most of the time, these patterns are not obvious to the person involved, making it difficult to see what is happening, let alone to do something about it.

So, I'll ask again. Why do they keep signing up for the same mistreatment from the next person? The same form of abuse or neglect, or maybe a new one?

From my understanding, there are a few reasons why someone might find themselves repeating a negative relationship pattern.

One scenario is because an individual is attracted to drama, and yet another is because someone has an addictive personality. In both cases, the individual appears to feed off the attention and excitement created by the constant upheaval in the relationship.

However, neither of these describe my situation. I am not drawn to drama or negativity and certainly do not like the attention it attracts. Nor do I have an addictive personality, thankfully.

Therefore, I needed to look further to discover the source behind my predicament. And, after a lot of careful scrutiny, I found it.

My analysis leads me to believe that if the social lifeline of experiences is followed back far enough, there is a strong possibility it will point to a pivotal person in the individual's past.

The person might have been a parent, sibling, aunt or uncle. Maybe they were a neighbor, teacher or classmate. In truth, their relationship status is irrelevant. The fact is that they were someone who left their indelible mark on the individual by how they treated them.

Oftentimes, it was a person the individual looked up to and admired. In some instances, possibly someone on whom they had a crush. In any of these cases though, it was most likely someone whose acceptance and approval they sought.

Yet other possibilities exist, such as someone fleeting in their life who stole a moment to rape or otherwise brutally attack the physical being or emotional integrity of the individual. Such an attack could haunt them, making it difficult to trust again and love openly.

Specifics will vary, but the point remains that most people in these patterns do not *choose* to be. Instead, I believe it reverts to something of which they are probably unaware. Something that dictates what they understand themselves to be worthy of, and deep down inside, they believe.

After these frustrating experiences, it was my sister, Jacqueline, who made a vital observation about my relationships. We were talking on the phone one afternoon, when she shared her thoughts.

"I've been thinking and I hope I don't offend you, but I feel like I need to bring it up. I know how hard you try to make it work with your boyfriends, but I can't help but wonder how you've wound up in a pattern of negative relationships. You're very passionate and giving. It doesn't make sense," she said.

"Wow, well, thank you for the compliment. You know, Jaye, I hadn't realized I was in a pattern."

"I know you didn't choose to be, but I hope you'll think about it and see if you can break it. You deserve to be in a loving relationship. Samantha and I have the same parents and background, and we've married wonderful men who truly love us. It just makes me wonder . . ."

"I'm grateful you brought it up. I'll think about it. If nothing else, I feel better knowing it may not all be my fault," I said, thanking her for her compassion as we ended our call.

Knowing she despises confrontation, I knew that conversation was difficult for her. I was moved by her concern and realized her suggestion gave me hope. Maybe I could indeed break the pattern, and I already had an idea where to begin.

Now it was my turn to go on account and become the pirate of my own soul. It had been plundered and pillaged enough. With respect to making it whole again and protecting it from other pirates, I decided it was time to steal it back, in its entirety, once and for all.

I was facing a gale-force wind and prepared for the rough seas ahead. I was determined to succeed and break the pattern of how I had been treated by the majority of the men in my life, as well as countless other individuals.

My soul searching commenced, starting off in high gear. My analytical nature was happy to be put to task and it was fitting to do a full review. To explain this, I must tell you the fundamental issue had persisted for decades.

If I chose to proceed, I needed to address certain truths from my past. Somehow, I would have to revisit the underlying source controlling my tolerance for, and selection of, negative romantic relationships.

I realized that if I were to finally be free, I needed to unravel myself from the multitude of knots into which I had been tied. Now, with a full understanding of how deeply entwined this had become, starting my quest was of paramount importance.

Chapter 41

Return to the Mainland

Several months after ending the relationship with Plan B, I was still single. Things went haywire with the economy and I seized the opportunity to take a break from my Florida life without incurring unnecessary financial repercussions. At the end of spring, I closed up my home and returned to my folks' place to maintain things during their three-month vacation.

I was excited to have the privacy of their expansive property along with the time and mental space to chill out. The upkeep of the gardens, lawn and pool was therapeutic, providing a wonderful change of pace. Feeling refreshed in the countryside, the hustle and bustle of South Florida became a distant memory as I focused on my chores.

When they returned, Mom asked if I was going to stay or head back to Florida. I knew Dad would be disgruntled if I stayed, but I wasn't ready to leave. Therefore, I told her it depended on whether or not I could find a job.

Two days later, despite the dreadful economy, I landed a part-time job at a local establishment. As fate would have it, I would be residing in Michigan for an undetermined amount of time.

The economy steadily worsened as the months ticked by and I was struggling to make a dime. I lived off my savings, keeping the Florida place going and trying to stay afloat in Michigan. Although my parents allowed me to stay with them, expenses were eating through my savings like sugar gnawing through tooth enamel, creating a cavity I have yet to fill.

To add to my financial frustration, my father's mood and disposition toward my presence was undeniable. His resentment grew daily while he filled Mom's head with his version of what I was doing with my time.

One afternoon, pursuant to one such conversation with Dad, she joined me at the dining room table where I had been working on the computer all day. As if reading my mind, she set two cups of coffee on the table and took a seat. I thanked her and took a sip, wondering what she wanted to discuss.

"Honey, your dad and I are concerned. We're happy to have you here, but need to know how you're spending your time. He says you're playing computer games all day, rather than looking for work."

I sighed, wondering why I was always defending myself against ill-founded speculations. It was disheartening and frustrating that certain people in the family assumed the worst about me and shared their tainted views with anyone available to listen. Once again, I had to disprove the rumor.

"Really? Yes, I'm on the computer all day. I'm either looking for more work or designing marketing materials for my current job. He'd know this, if he asked me rather than say stuff to make you doubt me. Here, see the employment ads?" I asked, turning the computer toward her. "Would you like to see the brochures I created? Maybe if you see what I've been doing, you'll see that I'm telling the truth," I said, opening the files.

"I don't doubt you; your father brought it up to me." She sighed as she pulled her chair in closer for a better look. "I can see the detail you've put into everything. They're very professional and I hope they bring you business," she said, taking a sip of her coffee.

"Thanks, Mom. I'm sorry if my being here is an imposition. If I'm causing problems, just tell me and I'll head south."

"No, don't worry about it. I'll set him straight and let him know you're doing what you can to find more work."

"Okay, thank you," I said, wrapping my hands around the coffee mug to warm them. "I just wish he'd stop assuming the worst of me and give me the benefit of the doubt once in a while. If nothing else, at least ask me what he needs to know, rather than post accusations. When have I purposefully caused him grief?" I asked, pushing the computer aside.

"I don't know," she said, sighing again. "I know what you're saying, but don't know how to make him see you differently than he does ..."

She had heard this sort of thing too many times over the years and I knew it crushed her. After all, this was not the first dispute between us where she found herself in the middle.

However, we both knew she couldn't influence how Dad viewed me. Any changes to his perception had to start with him, or it was not going to happen.

I didn't know where it stemmed from and never understood why he treated me differently from my sisters. I was not a daughter a father should be ashamed of or disgusted with, but he acted as though I were. Over the course of many years, I tried to understand his disapproval of me to know how to address or fix it, but never succeeded.

Luckily, during this time in Michigan, both Mom and Jacqueline saw his reactions toward me, if and when he chose to acknowledge me. His attitude troubled them enough to mention it and, although I was glad they witnessed it, I responded truthfully that it was normal.

After all this time, I was used to it. In the past, I had mentioned it to other adults in the family, but no one knew what I was referring to. This, along with how he regularly treated me, was what I fought continuously but apparently eluded everyone else.

You may notice the parallel between Casanova, Rebound Man, and Plan B and how they were able to fool others while privately undermining my self-esteem. This pattern of tolerance began here, with my father.

However, now that it had been identified, it would end with me.

The magnificent season of fall and its stunning, colorful glory came and went quickly and winter dragged on, colder than ever. It was an extreme change from Florida, but I delighted in the beauty of the snow and sheer crispness of the cold air.

I was wearing an average of four layers when I left the house and oddly, I enjoyed it. I was embracing winter for the first time and having fun getting to know family and friends better.

I reflected on my relationships and how fortunate I was to have had this time to deepen my bond with Mom. I knew it was a rare opportunity that money could not buy. If nothing else evolved from the past several months, that alone would make my return to the mainland priceless.

Winter was on its way out when I realized I had been home for close to a year. Even though I was working and enjoying myself socially, I felt unproductive with my time. My bank account was nearly empty and debt was rapidly accumulating on my credit cards.

In addition to that grim fact, Dad's attitude was as heavy and relentless as the persistently rainy, cold, gray days. Considering these details, I questioned why I was still there. With winter behind us and spring upon us, I knew I needed to make a decision.

At this time, I was planning to go to Florida in early May to be a bridesmaid in my friend's wedding. But I also needed to consider what to do going forward. Would I return to Michigan after her wedding? If not, then it was time to head south and begin again before her big day.

After a lot of thought and a long talk with Mom over a tall cup of hot cocoa and butterscotch schnapps, I decided to return to Florida. She offered to take my things in the van, and asked Jacqueline to accompany her on the drive. The date was set and a plan was in motion.

The day drew near for my return voyage. I put everything back into boxes and hauled them downstairs. Baby Goose, my Bengal pride and joy who traveled north with me last spring, sensed we were on the move again.

While I loaded the vehicles, he brought his toys to the pile. Pacing, he waited to see what was next, making sure he would not be left behind. The mood was somber; change was in the air.

The next morning, Mom and Jacqueline settled into the van and Goose and I moved into my car. We were ready and waiting to go, when in the final moments before leaving, Dad needed to talk to the two of them.

He leaned in through the driver's side window and chatted for several minutes. When he was finished, he went inside and we left.

He did not glance in my direction and never even said goodbye. He had chosen to ignore me again.

It was as though I did not exist.

Chapter 42

Too Familiar Territory

I cried from the driveway to the highway. My kitty sat in the passenger seat, silently reassuring me with adoring looks that we did not need kind, loving words from him to move forward in our lives. It was a good thing too, because it probably would have given the man a coronary if he had to utter a few.

When we pulled in to rest for the evening, Jacqueline and Mom mentioned what happened. I heard their concern, knowing they saw how often he treated me with contempt. My sister chose her words carefully, easing into a sore subject as gracefully as she could.

"Kendyl, Mom and I were discussing Dad's behavior toward you this morning. We've noticed it a lot this past year, but today was heartbreaking."

"Yes, well, it's nothing new, Jaye," I said wearily. "He's always been that way toward me. I'm surprised no one has caught on before now."

"I'm sorry that we didn't, and I'm sure you're right," Mom said as her voice cracked and tears began to form. "I know you've mentioned things in the past, but I never saw it until these past few months. He's been so obvious, it would've been impossible to miss."

"Don't worry about it, Mom," I said, realizing how much it hurt her. "It's not your fault, and you're not responsible for what he does. You shouldn't feel guilty. He's a pro at choosing his moments."

"No," Jaye said. "Something must be done, this can't continue. He's completely out of line with you. I mentioned it to Mom this afternoon, and we think the family should go for counseling."

"Thanks for wanting to help," I said, sighing. "I hope you know that I'm not the instigator. I won't make it hard for us to get along if he decides to try, but I don't need to be there."

"Alright, I'll keep you posted," she said.

It had been a long day and I was exhausted. I was pleased to have their support, but too tired to continue the discussion. I suggested going to dinner and making it an early night, and they both agreed. After dinner, we turned in for a solid night's rest.

We left the hotel the following morning and arrived at my place by midday. They helped unpack, and then prepared to depart the next day for their prompt return to Michigan. The next morning arrived too soon and it was difficult watching them leave, knowing I would be left to forge ahead alone once again.

With no time to waste, I began organizing everything to kick-start my life. I finished unpacking and made a few phone calls to previous places of employment to see if they could use my services again. It was time to put the last year behind me and move forward, starting anew.

A few weeks after my return, I was talking to Jaye on the phone when she revealed another observation about my relationships.

"Kendyl, I've been thinking about how Dad treats you. This really bothers me, and I'm sorry I never noticed enough to say something before."

"I can't believe you're still thinking about it," I said. "I'm not sure it would've done any good if you had anyway. But, thanks for caring."

"No, he shouldn't be doing this to you. In fact, I've thought about it and I think *he* is why you've had so many unsuccessful relationships," she said, pausing a minute for the weight of her statement to sink in. "Think about it. He's always treated you so differently than me and Samantha, and we didn't wind up in emotionally abusive relationships. It makes sense to me, and I think you should consider that's where it started."

"You know, I thought so before. But when everyone said it was me, I figured they must be right. Although I couldn't see how, when I hadn't done anything. I've always assumed that men, including Dad, treat me the way they do because of something I've said or done to upset them."

"Of course you think that! Dad portrays you as the problem, but you aren't. I saw him start fights when nothing was wrong. He manipulated situations to make us believe you were the troublemaker. But this winter, we saw that you weren't doing anything to irritate him and he was still upset with you."

"You're really convinced of this, aren't you?" I asked.

"Yes, and I've set up a family counseling meeting and Dad agreed to go. It'll be at the first of June and I'll let you know what happens. I will bring this up if necessary, to make sure it's addressed."

"Thank you, Jaye. This means a lot, no matter what comes of it. Please keep me posted on whatever happens."

"I will, and know that I love you and I'm sorry you haven't found a man to treat you right. Maybe this will help, and soon you'll find someone to give you the love we all know you deserve."

"Thank you. I love you too," I said, holding back my tears as we said goodbye.

I was not used to people going to bat for me, and it was amazing to hear her determination. The outcome of the family meeting would be irrelevant if nothing came of it, but knowing she tried would always be with me.

Again, my mind was forced to wander into the past. I reflected on countless events of various levels of importance in my life where I knew Dad left his mark. I concluded I was not the disappointment he made me out to be.

Instead, I realized he never gave me a chance at anything. His answer to my requests for help or guidance throughout my youth and over the years was either "No," or "Ask your sister."

I remember specifically asking him one day if he would teach me how to drive a motorcycle. Everyone else in the family was adept at it and I wanted to learn, too. He had taught my sisters, and I was hopeful we could do it together and connect on something.

He did not lean on any excuses, such as not having time or the bike needing gas or repairs. Instead, he simply responded with his usual retort, "No. Go ask your sister."

"That is something a father should teach. *Not* a sister," I said, walking away.

My attempt to be a part of his life was defeated, again. Granted, my sister might have been more patient and easier to work with, but I wanted desperately to spend time with Dad and to learn from him.

The rejections were routine as he repeatedly pushed me away. He did not initiate friendly conversation, indicate an interest in me, or ask what I wanted to do with my life. He showed minimal concern in general, although he never hesitated to put me to work or dish out a punishment for whatever he thought I did wrong.

Adding all of this together, I eventually stopped asking him questions, for his help or input.

Interestingly, when someone becomes more independent, those who think they should still play a part in making their decisions or being a source to rely on, often bristle. You know the type, those who need to control everyone and everything around them.

I realized the men in my life did not want to help me directly, nor did they want me to be an independent thinker and make things happen for myself. They needed to feel like they were not only in control of the relationship, but also of me.

The need to control the relationship could also be considered a parallel. This example (sadly) brings six pirates to mind: Bad Boy, who felt the need to deny me and then save me from an awful fate; Driver, who refused to teach me or let others do the job; Money Man, who wanted me to be a kept woman; Rebound Man, who refused to help and disapproved of my success; and Casanova and Plan B, who used their moods to control the relationship whenever they felt threatened.

After this analysis, I concluded that I was an anomaly to my father. Okay, maybe an anomaly is being generous. Maybe I was viewed as more of a threat because I challenged him. But, considering how long it had been going on, I knew I wasn't being given a fair shot, either way.

I realized that rather than trying to understand me, he belittled and berated me, apparently anticipating this would put me in a place where he could control me. And yet another connection can be made from this observation directly to Driver, Rebound Man, and Plan B.

Further irritation developed when I did not submit and accept their destructive words as final. Anger surfaced and resentment grew when I questioned them directly or made adjustments to suit myself.

I remember one precise moment when I was twelve and this happened with Dad.

We were getting ready to go out to work in the fields. I was sifting through a drawer, looking for a pair of gloves. He was becoming impatient with me, as usual, because I was holding him up.

"I can't believe how stupid you are!" he exclaimed, his hand on the doorknob, ready to go.

"Your opinion of me doesn't matter," I said, without looking up.

In less than a second, he covered the space between us with a couple of long, determined strides. Hovering over me with flared nostrils, he sneered and yelled, "I am your father! My opinion of you had *better* matter!"

I remained unaffected as I slowly raised my gaze to meet his glare. "Not if that is your opinion of me," I said, looking him in the eye with the steadfast calm that typically precedes a tempest.

He huffed angrily, but said nothing as his eyes glowed hot with rage and his face flushed to a heated, deep shade of red. Immediately turning on his heel, he spun around and marched away as quickly as he had moved toward me moments ago. He left and slammed the door violently, causing the windows to shake throughout the house.

I found a matching pair of gloves and slowly made my way out to the field. As I walked along, I became sad as I tried to understand what would make a father speak poorly to a bright, ambitious, loving daughter.

This example is only one of such events that transpired between us.

What I like about who I was when I defended myself against his insulting words, is that I knew I was right, but not insolent. I knew I had the right, if not an obligation, to stand up for myself, and did it without fear.

When people speak to others in a disrespectful manner without cause, they should be prepared for the other person to respond accordingly, regardless of their status. I did not owe him kind words after his derogatory comment, and he should have expected nothing less than what he received.

I understood that age and relationship status are irrelevant details when discussing disrespect. Therefore, this was not a lack of respect on my part, but rather on his.

However, because his was a position of authority and he was not to be countered, some kind of punishment would follow. I quickly learned that if I did not quietly accept and tolerate his degrading words, there would be bigger problems.

By the time I became an adult, I had lost my edge in defending myself, knowing it always backfired. Although I never agreed with allowing myself to be trampled, I had learned to fear the consequences.

As such, there were many times in my adult relationships when the attitude required for self-protection was missing. I couldn't help but wonder where the brave and courageous girl went who understood its value.

I want her back.

She did not hesitate to state her case and stand up for herself when under attack. She knew her power was hers, not someone else's to steal because they had more money, were bigger, older, or in a position of control.

A scene pops into my mind that should help you understand how extreme he could be.

I was in high school. One afternoon after class, I came home distraught about something. I can't remember the cause of my anxiety, but I was an emotional wreck and went straight up to my room.

Closing the door softly, I threw myself onto the bed and buried my face in the pillow, sobbing my heart out. Although I purposefully chose the privacy and isolation of my bedroom to sort through my sorrows, my solitude was rudely disrupted.

Minutes later, my father raced up the stairs, threw the door open and shouted, "If you don't stop crying, I'll give you something to cry about! Now get up and go back downstairs!"

After his callous command, he left. I heard him stomp down the stairs as he retreated to the lower level. Quietly, I pulled it together and dried my tears.

Shocked by the attack and lying there in a state of vulnerability, I was defenseless and defeated. Unsure of what happened and why, I submitted to his demands, only to arrive downstairs without any further communication from him.

I never understood it, and I still don't. I did not impose on him, say anything to him, or give him any reason to come after me and demand I stop crying. My grief had nothing to do with him. Whatever I was experiencing was not about him and it was not his, but he would not allow me to have it, either.

This type of abuse is one I believe to be an ultimate form of control and is extremely destructive. I can draw a parallel here to my experience with Casanova after he went cold.

In addition, as a self-supporting adult, my father still chose not to participate in my life. He would sporadically rise to the occasion if necessary, but in general, he kept his distance.

Despite his refusal to participate and apparent lack of interest, he was determined to maintain his view of me. Somehow, he managed to form his opinions and regularly make judgments of how I was living and the decisions I made, which consequently did not impact him one way or the other.

Regardless of the facts, he already knew I was wrong or guilty, whatever the case. When this piece slid into place, it occurred to me that I was fighting a losing battle and I knew my analysis was complete.

Through the process of this review, it hit me. I summarized my relationships collectively and understood. Regardless of how I turned it, the guts and the gore of it all came down to one basic concept: *I had been seeking a man's acceptance, approval, and unconditional love since childhood.*

When a person has been wrongly judged and denied their entire life, they may not verbalize it. How they allow others to mow them over becomes testimony to the fact that somewhere deep inside, they either believe they deserve it, or have no idea how else they should expect to be treated.

I was no exception, even though I thought I should be treated better.

In general, my relationships started out well. Time passed before the subtle chiseling away at my personality would begin and eventually show. When the pirates became comfortable with the relationship, they seemed to need to control me and alter who I was or how I participated with others.

By then, I was emotionally invested and blind to their intentions. Instead, I was merely flowing in the direction I was nudged.

Although I would not outwardly conform to what a boyfriend wanted in a woman, plenty of concessions were provided. I can see via reflection how I tolerated what I now know to be emotional and verbal abuse, hoping he would treat me with love and respect.

I wanted him to genuinely love and embrace me for the person I was. I wanted a man to look at me with adoration and respect, support me in my dreams, and encourage me to become the best person I could be. Someone who appreciated me for me, rather than what I could do for him or how I could make him feel bigger or better about himself, while suffocating my spirit and stealing my soul.

What an incredible realization. What an epiphany!

Although I had previously wondered if things might have stemmed from my relationship with Dad, now I had a definitive answer.

I now understood why I was locked in a pattern of negative relationships and why I tolerated each of them for as long as I did. Thanks to Jaye's insight, I was on my path to breaking the pattern.

Shortly after my epiphany, she phoned with an update. The family had met with a pastor.

As was recounted to me, my father began revealing how he felt about me a few minutes into the meeting. My sister said she was glad I wasn't there, because much of the meeting revolved around his disapproval of me.

The pastor allowed Dad to talk, and then asked him one question. "So, is it that your daughter has chosen a lifestyle you don't approve of, or that you just don't like her?"

The beauty of the pastor's inquiry was simple. Regardless of how you turned it, any parent should be ashamed to be asked the question because a redeeming answer did not exist.

In addition, the pastor provided insight from a perspective my father could respect: a man's. I don't know if he answered the question, but the pastor had made his point.

Two weeks after the meeting, Jaye phoned again.

"Hey, it's me," she said. "Dad asked me to call. You know how the meeting went, well, he's thought about it. He wants to fly you home as a surprise for Mom and start making amends with you."

"That's great. Thanks for keeping me posted and for calling. Please tell Dad you're not going to do his dirty work for him. Tell him I refuse to let him use Mom as a pawn to get to me, and vice versa. If he wants to make amends, he can call me himself. After we've covered our territory, then we can discuss me visiting and us surprising Mom," I said, having no empathy for Dad.

"I don't blame you one bit. I'll let him know."

She sounded pleased with my stance on the subject and it was good to know she agreed. We talked about a few other things and then ended the conversation.

I admit I was both surprised by the gist of her call and also skeptical of his intentions. Playing with my hopes and emotions was something too many men had been allowed to do. Every time their thoughtless, selfish behavior led to my sadness and frustration, they continued on undisturbed.

This was too important to me, and too vital to my relationship with my father, for it to be taken lightly. If he meant it, then he would have to prove it.

In the past, he had called only once and it was for a family emergency. Therefore, if he did call, I would believe he was serious.

Two weeks later, the phone rang.

It was Dad.

Chapter 43

Parley

"Hi Kendyl, it's Dad. Sorry I haven't called sooner. I've been waiting for Mom to be in town so we could talk without distraction. I know Jackie told you, but I'm hoping to make amends with you."

"Thanks for calling, Dad, but I'm going to be honest. If you're calling to go through the motions to make Mom happy, then we can stop now and save time. However, if you're sincere and want a healthy relationship with me, then we can continue. It's up to you."

"I want to work this out," he said, sounding relieved.

By cutting through the nonsense to keep it real, I made it easier for both of us. Although he may not have known, I had spent decades wishing for my father to love and adore me the way he did my sisters.

Since my recent epiphany, I had worked through whatever emotions were lingering in the shadows. I sorted through the remnants amongst the tears of sadness, frustration, and anger all mixed together.

Now, with a clear mind and thoughts of my own which I intended to express during this rare opportunity, I was able to remain calm. I was not interested in turning this into an emotional battlefield where we would argue, place blame, keep score, or tear each other apart and gain nothing.

The past was the past, and what was done would always be. It was time to address underlying issues and move forward, starting from a clean slate.

It was time for a parley and I was ready.

"I've been thinking since our meeting a few weeks ago, and I'm sure you have some things to say about it," he said. I waited for him to continue, before assuming I knew where he was headed. "Anyway, after talking to your mom and Jackie, I know I've misjudged you. I want to work this out so we can go forward, if that's even possible."

"I'm willing to work on it if you are, but you have to mean it. You can't say this just to make things right with Mom. That won't work," I said at the risk of sounding redundant.

"I know. I'm serious and promise to make things right. So, I know you heard about the meeting. Do you have anything you want to discuss or questions you want to ask?"

"I do. I've had plenty of time, years in fact, to think about this, and have a few things to discuss. I'll stick to the pertinent issues," I said, grabbing my coffee and taking a seat. If we were going to have a serious discussion, then I was going to get comfortable. I took a sip and settled in.

"Okay, I'm listening," he said quietly.

"I want to know why you've always treated my sisters with so much more compassion than me. Why you can help them when they ask for help, but when I ask, you send me to someone else, brushing me off like a nuisance. What is there about me that makes you want to create and maintain a wedge between us? What have I done that you don't want me around you?"

A heavy sigh followed this first, loaded inquiry.

"I don't know," he said. "Well, there hasn't been anything you've done. I don't think I was aware I treated you differently or brushed you off. But I know I have, because Jackie and your mom pointed out instances to me. I honestly don't have a good answer for you, honey. I know you deserve something more concrete, but I really don't have it."

"Okay, I can accept that. But, can you tell me now that you'll be more conscious of how you treat me in the future?"

"Absolutely."

"Good. I've been able to rise above most of it, but knowing you're willing to work on it is a welcome relief," I said, grateful to have the first issue behind us. "On another note, why do you pass judgment about me without asking any questions? You always assume the worst, telling Mom stuff you make up about me without the facts. And, sort of in the same box, why are you so disappointed with me? How have I failed so miserably, that you're that unhappy with me?"

"You haven't," he said thoughtfully. "I guess I expected you to be more successful, knowing you have the potential. I suppose my disappointment stems from the fact that you don't use your degree."

"Well, you can say that if you want, but we both know this started long before I went to college. And, I did use my degree, but was permanently laid off. The recession made it impossible to get a job in my field. Afterward, along with moving to Florida, my education was obsolete.

"There are extenuating circumstances which I had no control over. Yet, I had to figure out how to overcome them on my own and it seems that even having done so, you've neglected to give me any credit. You're very good at assuming the worst, no matter how hard I try."

"I suppose you have a point, but I didn't have all the facts," he said, sighing heavily.

"That's part of what I'm saying, Dad. You don't have all the facts. You base your decisions about me and how to treat me on your assumptions, and you always assume the worst about me. I can't win no matter what I do, because you've already made up your mind," I said, pleased to have expressed this without unnecessary emotion built into it.

"I never thought about it like that," he said.

I waited for him to continue, knowing he was reflecting on everything laid out before him. After several moments, he responded with intense emotion, the strain in his voice audible through the line.

"I'm sorry, Kendyl. You're right. I never have given you the chance to prove otherwise, and I see that now."

"Just talk to me, Dad. Express an interest in me and my life."

"I'd like that," he said. "I don't know why I haven't tried it before. I guess I assumed you'd rather talk to your mom about everything instead.

"Well, now you know I'd love to talk to both of you," I said and smiled, hoping he could hear it through the phone.

With these issues addressed, I felt the tension ease on the other end of the line. We continued talking for over two hours. It was amazing and remains one of the few things I pinpoint in my life as a personal miracle.

My father persisted throughout the call in ways I would never have imagined. He opened doors willingly, through which he might have suspected anger to follow, allowing himself to be interrogated further.

He listened and answered my questions. He expressed sorrow and grief for treating me the way he had and there was sincere remorse in his tone. At one point, I knew he was frustrated with the cards stacking against him when he realized what he was being held accountable for.

"Kendyl, I ... I can't change the past."

"I know you can't, and I'm not asking you to," I said. "However, I am asking you to pay attention to avoid repeating the pattern. I wouldn't mention it now if it wasn't relevant, but it is because you still do it. It isn't what happened or the frequency of occurrence, so much as the marks left behind. You can make sure it doesn't happen again."

"I will, and am relieved to hear you say that," he said. "That's the outcome I want from today. Until they pointed things out, I didn't know what I was doing. I realize that sounds like an excuse, but now that I see what I've done and how much I've hurt you and Mom, I want it to stop."

The conversation continued on a lighter note. I asked for the chance to be the person I am, rather than a disappointment based on assumptions. He not only readily agreed, but also provided a sincere, heartfelt apology.

After we worked through the issues I felt needed to be discussed, I introduced him to his daughter. He listened intently and asked several questions throughout my debut.

I told him about my goals and current projects. He was surprised to learn of my ambition and excited to see what I was working on the next time I visited.

When the conversation was coming to a close, I had one more question to ask. I tried to avoid it, but knew this was the time to bring it up, and it had nagged at me for decades.

It was the only thing I could think of as to why he raised me the way he had. Refusing me my emotions and always forcing me to figure things out on my own, brushing me aside while saving his empathy and tenderness for my sisters. The time had come, and I needed to know.

"Dad, I have one more question to ask, and I need you to be honest in your response," I said, now pacing the floor.

"Yes, of course. What is it?"

"Were you disappointed I was born a girl, and not a boy?" I asked before I could change my mind.

Silence flooded the airwaves between us. A long, strained moment that felt like forever, followed the question. When he finally spoke, I heard his voice break as he choked out the words. I knew without a doubt he was crushed to have been asked but understood my reasoning, which saddened him further.

"No…absolutely not. I'm so sorry I ever made you feel that way…"

And there it was, the number one answer I needed to hear. It was not the reason behind his actions after all, which gave me hope.

I know we were both relieved to have the talk behind us and emerged on the other side in better shape than when we went in. We covered new ground together and arrived in a new territory. We established a new path, one clear of debris and useless emotional clutter.

When I set him free of the obligation to fix the past, I think it gave him a new perspective on my ability to reason. In addition, I think he realized he would not be weighed down with unnecessary guilt or blame that could never serve a higher purpose.

A few weeks after our chat, he flew me in to surprise Mom. He picked me up from the airport with tears in his eyes and a massive hug of love. We arrived at the house and sat talking for a while before Mom returned from town.

He has since become a present father, one whom I can turn to for advice and comfort, as well as simple talks and silly stories. And, the best part is that he is no longer just a father.

He is now truly my dad.

Chapter 44

Resting at Harbor

The day of our talk was an amazing day for me, one I will never forget and always cherish. I know some people will question Dad's sincerity. Some will believe I exaggerated for my own sake, and others will doubt that it happened.

For those of you who do believe, you will understand the depth and value that can come from a gift such as this. The blessing of being given a second chance with my father before it was too late, simply cannot be put into words.

I must suggest if someone has influenced your life in a similar way but you cannot address it with them for reasons out of your control, then please do yourself the favor of forgiving them. It will, in time, set *you* free.

I know most people will not have the opportunity for an experience like the one I shared with you. I am also aware it wouldn't have happened without the help of certain key players.

On that note, I must say thank you to Mom for her continuous support through everything. To my sister, I say thank you for her determination and willingness to intervene. If she had not been adamant about the meeting, I doubt Dad and I would have had our talk. To the pastor, I say thank you for his accurate observations that caused Dad to think things over.

And to my father, I say thank you for wanting to make amends with me, following through, and then for keeping his promise. Because he was willing to acknowledge his role in our relationship and also determined to fix it, I now have a father whom I am pleased to call my dad.

Our parley happened several years ago as of this writing, and we are doing well. We have an open line of communication wherein either may call to discuss whatever, whenever.

And now, I believe I have a stronger and more powerful relationship with him than I would have had otherwise. I am also a different person than if he had been softer, kinder, and more loving toward me. Granted, it might have led to healthier relationships from the beginning, but maybe that would have taken me away from the course I was supposed to follow.

Maybe I was supposed to experience these things to have something to write about and share with others, hopefully helping them understand some of the patterns in their own lives. Quite possibly, I would not have had recent conversations with Dad that led him to take action where needed, creating more positive results.

Then again, maybe the collective purpose of my experiences was to help me find my ground, discover my true level of determination, and ultimately, stand up for myself. Maybe it is a combination of things.

Regardless of the reasons, I know the relationships and experiences from my past have prepared me for my future. They have each contributed to my strength, wisdom, and independence.

Because of them, I am more determined and self-sufficient than before, yes, but I have not been hardened into an insensitive, uncaring individual. They have broadened my understanding of my tenacity to be who I am and what it means to fight to preserve my own self-worth—and that I must.

Upon review of my past relationship with my father and the dominating, destructive, degrading tendencies in the men I dated for the majority of my adulthood, I can see the pattern and how it developed.

My desire to have a healthy, accepting relationship with him dictated the lack of acceptance I felt. Subconsciously, it created a tolerance which then transferred to the romantic man in my life. This provided access to my vulnerabilities, allowing him to become a pirate and quietly steal my soul.

I know now that although I was fighting for who I was, my father acted as the dominant force in my life. He was also the one I looked to the most for approval and to applaud my accomplishments.

But instead of supporting and encouraging me, he pushed me aside and forced me into a box. Shutting me out, he denied me my emotions, told me to stay quiet, keep my opinions to myself and accept things as they were without question.

Through it all, he succeeded at forcing me to put the best parts of who I am into a chest, buried deep at the back of the closet. Imagine my surprise when I found it, opened it up and saw my true self, my soul, waiting to be embraced and worn proudly again.

Coincidentally, after each relationship reached its termination, I re-visited my secret treasure chest. Inside, I always found my most valuable personality assets, set aside for the pirate's personal security. My sense of humor, self-confidence, self-worth, independence, and desire to succeed were all there.

However, since my epiphany, I no longer find pieces of me inside this chest. Now, I only find the doubloons and pieces of eight representing the pirates and lessons learned from them.

I know that how I was treated was unacceptable to me and although I thank each pirate for the lessons they taught, as well as my father for making amends, that does not excuse their behavior.

And because I cannot change others, I chose to focus on what I could do to improve the quality of my life and relationships going forward. I took the time and did my homework, completing my transformational voyage to find my power.

Throughout this process, I successfully broke the pattern and have not dated a pirate since Plan B. Additionally, and, most importantly, I gained a positive relationship with my dad.

When I look back, I see how everything came together to make the shift happen for me to move forward and have healthier relationships. Naturally, I didn't see it at the time, but now it makes sense that I needed to leave home to create the space for change to occur. Apparently, I needed to repeat this part of the process a few times before the timing would be right for the pieces to fall into place.

I have healed from the damage created by the pirates of my soul, each and every one of them.

Finally, I am resting at harbor.

And now, with all of this behind me, I am ready for the man who will become the captain of my heart.

The one who, unlike those who came before, will never try to steal my soul.

Epilogue

Are you in an abusive relationship? Are you in a pattern of abusive or negative relationships? If you are, then beware, a pirate is probably stealing your soul!

But what if you are unsure? How can you tell?

If you question whether or not you're falling into a similar pattern, then please continue reading.

The pirates are listed here to help you identify with their personality traits. As you read through each one, you will see the undeniable pattern forming.

Following each pirate's description is a list of questions pertaining to his typical personality traits or relationship style. These questions are provided for you to ask yourself about the relationship(s) you have in your own life.

If you find yourself answering "Yes" to the majority of the questions beneath a certain pirate, then you may be in a relationship similar to the one I described with him. Although your relationships will vary from mine, the underlying tone may be the same.

The lists, as well as the questions, are not all-inclusive. They are a general guideline, and provide a starting point for discerning the types of relationships possible, if at least a majority of them are present. Please note that this approach is based solely on my observation and analysis. It is neither foolproof, nor scientific, and may not apply to you.

If you decide to read through each pirate's list, you will notice similarities between them and the accompanying list of questions. Questions reappearing under multiple pirates support the evidence of a pattern forming.

By the time you reach the last entry, that of Plan B, you will notice his list includes more than any other pirate. To me, this indicates how deep I was into the pattern.

You will also notice that, although the pirates had positive traits, I focus solely on the negative. This is because it is challenging to be honest about a relationship while remembering only what we thought was good.

This exercise is meant to broaden your mind and open your eyes, if necessary. The summaries provided might lead you to understand possible issues in your own relationship. To be fair, one must look at all parties involved and assign responsibility wherever they apply.

That being said, please be honest with yourself. Consider what role you could be playing, if any, in whatever concerns you might have.

Be willing to acknowledge if you are attracted to negative relationships because you need the drama or thrive on the attention they provide. Or, if you are addicted to this kind of relationship, ask yourself if you want to resolve the matter and if so, consider asking for help.

Regardless of your situation, know that if you want to improve it, you can.

In addition, please be willing to step up your game to be a better partner, as well as to stand up for yourself, because both are equally important to achieve a healthy relationship of mutual love and respect.

I trust that my story, this experiment, and any self-analysis or understanding derived from any portion of this book is understood to be a tool that may help with self-awareness. Please understand that I am not telling you what to do or what is best for you. Only you can make that decision.

Additionally, I would never suggest or imply that you should endanger yourself or others in any way (physically, emotionally, financially, etc.). If that is a possibility, please find applicable professional assistance.

And now, my dear reader, I leave the rest to you.

Bad Boy

aimless, controlling, dominating, lazy, manipulative, mean-spirited, rebellious, victim, vindictive, violent

1. Were they financially capable (or appear to be) when you met them, yet now need your ongoing financial assistance?

2. Are they always in between jobs, seeking employment or losing their job? Are they complacent and content letting you pull the load?

3. Do they have an excuse for everything or blame their circumstances on others, always playing the role of the victim?

4. Are they always looking for a fight or quick to start one (verbal or physical)?

5. Do they become temperamental when you ask personal questions?

6. Are they physically destructive and violent?

7. Do you find yourself taking care of them and feeling more like their parent than their lover?

8. Do they have something they are working on or several opportunities for income, but never any results? Do they always have money coming, but need to borrow until it does (and never pay)?

9. Do they create negative situations and then fix them or save you from them, to be the hero?

Driver

arrogant, condescending,
controlling, detached, self-absorbed

1. Do your activities together primarily (or always) rotate around what they want to do?

2. Do you have to find someone else to accompany you or go alone for activities you want to do because they refuse to do what you want?

3. Do they become irritated when someone else is willing to help you with something they will not do with or for you?

4. Do they exclude you from important aspects or people in their life?

5. Do they refuse to help you when you need assistance or if they do help, is it done grudgingly?

6. Do they speak down to you, especially in front of others?

7. Do they say hurtful things to or about you and pretend it is supposed to be funny?

8. Do they insinuate you do not measure up by their comments and innuendos, implying you are not their equal?

9. Do they act superior to you? Do they make you feel like you will never be good enough for them?

10. Is it more important to have you appear on their arm, than to be part of the conversation? In other words, are you meant to decorate but stay quiet?

Money Man

arrogant, controlling, dictating, manipulative,
possessive, scheming, selfish, vengeful, vindictive

1. Are they always trying to buy their way into your affections and out of situations?

2. Do they expect full access to you and your home when you have not offered it?

3. Are they pushing you for something you are not ready to give?

4. Is it more important to have you appear on their arm, than to be part of the conversation? In other words, are you meant to decorate but stay quiet?

5. Do they complain about your work or chosen lifestyle?

6. Are they too eager to marry you or make it known that you belong to them?

7. Do they become frustrated when you do not eagerly receive either gifts or lifestyle options they offer to you?

8. Do they offer you things that, if accepted, would take away a piece of your independence or compromise your integrity?

9. Do they insist on you participating with their acquaintances, but never willingly participate with yours?

10. Does everything they do for you feel like they have an ulterior motive? Do they seem to always have a hidden agenda?

11. Do they behave like a spoiled brat when they do not get their way?

12. Do they become vindictive when you stand up for yourself?

13. Do they become vengeful when you withdraw or retreat?

14. Do they try to change you?

Casanova

controlling, detached, emotionally unavailable,
manipulative, mean-spirited, passive-aggressive, selfish

1. Do your activities together primarily (or always) rotate around what they want to do?

2. Do they seem overly pleased, even gloating, when they know they have hurt your feelings?

3. Do they make statements or promises and not follow through, yet become irritated when you ask about it?

4. Do they expect you to geographically move, change jobs or friends to be with them while maintaining their own life and not suggesting, initiating or being willing to discuss any compromise?

5. Do you feel like you have to tiptoe around them, making sure you do not upset them most or all the time?

6. Does their mood dictate yours, events you both attend, or the time you spend together?

7. Do they push your buttons to upset you, watching for a reaction and when you have one, make you feel guilty for reacting?

8. Do they dictate which emotions you are allowed to have and when?

9. Do they exclude you from people and activities in their life?

10. Do they use intimacy as a tool to get what they want in the relationship?

11. Do they say they love you, yet treat you with indifference?

12. Do they initiate and maintain silent treatments for days for no apparent reason?

13. Do you frequently find yourself questioning what you have said or done to upset them?

14. Do they act like they would rather be alone than in the relationship with you?

15. Are they emotionally closed or unavailable? Do they shut you out?

16. Do they set you up to fail?

Mon Homme

addict, angry, self-destructive, violent

1. Do they have an addiction?

2. Do they require regular use of a drug or illegal substance to appear stable or happy?

3. Do they frequently lie, cheat or steal?

4. Do they become irate and irrational instantly, without having been externally provoked? Do they have frequent, abrupt mood swings?

5. Are they physically destructive and violent? Do they ever raise a hand to you, push you or throw things at you?

6. Do they threaten you personally?

7. Do they repeatedly accuse you of things you did not do?

8. Do they have trust issues with you (and not because of something you have said or done)?

9. Are they always looking for a fight or quick to start one (verbal or physical)?

10. Do you see a distinct difference in their personality when they are sober, versus when they have been drinking or using drugs?

Rebound Man

condescending, controlling, jealous, manipulative,
passive-aggressive, possessive, selfish, victim, vindictive

1. Do they speak down to you, especially in front of others?

2. Do they readily mention other people's beauty or attractiveness to you and purposefully not compliment you on yours?

3. Do they sing other people's praises when they do or say something great, yet snuff you when you have your shining moments?

4. Do they generally assume the worst about what you say or do?

5. Does their mood dictate yours, events you both attend, or the time you spend together?

6. Is everything a competition between you?

7. Do they say or imply things meant to keep you in your place and under their control (such as for a woman, in the home)?

8. Do they treat you as though you have nothing of value to say or contribute?

9. Are they only capable of focusing on their own wants and needs?

10. Do they seem overly pleased, even gloating, when they know they have hurt your feelings?

11. Do they like to put you in your place?

12. Are they possessive of you and your time?

13. Do they try to make you jealous, either genuinely or for a reaction to which they can then initiate an argument?

14. Do they push your buttons to upset you, watching for a reaction and when you have one, make you feel guilty for reacting?

15. Are they determined to defeat you, even if it affects them negatively?

16. Do they dictate what you should wear or who your friends should be?

17. Are they overly jealous?

18. Do they set you up to fail?

Leech

aimless, con man, deceitful,
irresponsible, lazy, manipulative, selfish, victim

1. Do they become angry when you are not available to do something that they want?

2. Are they wandering through life looking for someone to support them?

3. Do they include you in fun activities only to share expenses, fill a seat, carry their luggage, or clean up?

4. Were they financially capable (or appear to be) when you met them, yet now need your ongoing financial assistance?

5. Do they expect you to meet their needs and take care of them, yet leave you to fend for yourself?

6. Are they, or were they, extremely eager to move into your place?

7. Do they expect you to pay for shared activities and evenings out or at least go Dutch every time?

8. Does their mood dictate yours, events you both attend, or the time you spend together?

9. Are they only capable of focusing on their own wants and needs?

10. Do they sulk or have a tantrum when they miss playtime?

11. Do they act helpless and pathetic?

12. Do they have something they are working on or several opportunities for income, but never any results? Do they always have money coming, but need to borrow until it does (and never pay)?

13. Do they lie regularly and create excuses for sympathy?

14. Do they have an excuse for everything or blame their circumstances on others, always playing the role of the victim?

15. Do you find yourself taking care of them and feeling more like their parent than their lover?

16. Do they make statements or promises and not follow through, yet become irritated when you ask about it?

17. Do they try to push their responsibilities or obligations onto you?

Plan B

controlling, deceitful, detached, manipulative,
mean-spirited, passive-aggressive, selfish, vindictive

1. Are they defensive when you ask about the relationship status, friends, and work (topics most couples discuss)?

2. Do you feel like you have to tiptoe around them, making sure not to upset them most or all the time?

3. Does their mood dictate yours, events you both attend, or the time you spend together?

4. Do you avoid topics of conversation to keep the peace, prevent arguments or being accused of causing problems?

5. Do you hold your tongue rather than defend yourself when belittled? Doing so to avoid confrontation or embarrassment in front of others, possible silent treatments, threats, accusations or physical abuse?

6. Do they want to spend time with you only when convenient for them?

7. Do they expect you to meet their needs and take care of them, yet leave you to fend for yourself? And do they always say "No" when you ask them for help?

8. Is everything a competition between you?

9. Do they like to put you in your place?

10. Do they often dismiss your opinions or input, especially in front of others?

11. Do you frequently find yourself questioning what you have said or done to upset them?

12. Do they always find fault with you, your work, interests or how you take care of yourself, home or children? And do they frequently correct or reprimand you, especially in front of others?

13. Do they readily mention other people's beauty or attractiveness to you and purposefully not compliment you on yours?

14. Do they sing other people's praises when they do or say something great, yet snuff you when you have your shining moments?

15. Do they often ask you to change something about yourself, be it your appearance, style, behavior, etc.?

16. Do they make statements or promises and not follow through, yet become irritated when you ask about it?

17. Do they generally assume the worst about what you say or do?

18. Do they try to make you jealous, either genuinely or for a reaction to which they can then initiate an argument?

19. Do they push your buttons to upset you, watching for a reaction and when you have one, make you feel guilty for reacting?

20. Do they lie regularly and are they genuinely dishonest?

21. Are they only capable of focusing on their own wants and needs?

22. Do they initiate and maintain silent treatments for days for no apparent reason?

23. Are they emotionally closed or unavailable? Do they shut you out?

24. Do they set you up to fail?

Whew! What a list. Did you notice how it grew? Sadly, this is to be expected when the lesson has not been learned. Once the lesson is learned however, better decisions can be made and improvement awaits.

Following are several questions (list not all-inclusive) that if answered with a "Yes," might indicate you are in a *positive* relationship. Especially if a significant number of the negative questions above are not mixed in as well.

Review them and evaluate whether or not these details are important to you. If they are, but missing from your relationship(s), then think about how you feel about living without them.

And, if you want to, add some of your preferences to the list. Think about what matters to you and jot it down.

Now, ask yourself how the absence of these positive things might impact you, your relationship and your life, versus finding a relationship where they are present and how it could empower you to be your best self.

Not a Pirate

1. Do they encourage you to pursue your dreams and set new goals?

2. Do they listen to you when you need to vent or express yourself, whether pertaining to your relationship or some other matter?

3. Are they emotionally available and invested in the relationship?

4. Do they want the same things out of life that you do?

5. If they live with you, do they contribute fairly and willingly?

6. Are they willing to compromise and meet you halfway?

7. Do they want to know your friends and family? Do they introduce you to theirs?

8. Do they give you physical affection, hugs, kisses and hand-holding?

9. Do they show they care about you and whatever (and whomever) is important to you?

10. Do they give you compliments, speaking kindly to and about you?

11. Do they offer to help when they see you struggling (emotionally or physically)?

12. Do they take care of you when you are ill?

13. Do they include you in their life and lifestyle?

14. Do they love you and do they act like it?

15. Do they let you be you?

We all know the perfect person is a myth. However, the idea is to find someone who is most suitable for us and our advancement through life.

Throughout your search for a healthy relationship, remember that it is important to understand that how we allow others to treat us on an ongoing basis is *our* responsibility first, not theirs.

I can honestly tell you that the men I dated who stole my soul, or any piece of it, were only able to because I unwittingly allowed it to happen.

If you see your reflection within my tale, then it's possible that you might have allowed someone to steal the true essence of you. Know that you have the power within you—and the right—to steal it back.

Just like I did.

Wishing you the best on your personal voyage,

Kendyl

Acknowledgments

I am grateful to family and friends who provide support while I pursue my path. Special thanks go to Mom for always being there for me and to my sister for her love, insight, and determination.

I wish to thank my first readers, Julia, Dot, Helen, and Linda. They each offered encouragement, input, and valuable suggestions. Their ongoing support, contributions, and enthusiasm are treasured for the constant motivation they provide.

And to all who read this, I thank you and hope you love it!

About the Author

Kendyl Jameson writes about her experiences and what she learned from them. She hopes by sharing with others, she can empower readers to live their best lives.

In addition to *The Pirates of My Soul: A Transformational Voyage to Self-Empowerment*, she is currently writing practical guides pertaining to credit and money. The first of which, *DIY Credit Repair: Beginners' Guide to Credit Repair*, is available in English and Spanish. Please visit amazon.com to purchase.

These guides are also based on her previous experiences. They are written with the intention of helping others build, fix, and maintain a healthy credit score, while learning how to understand the concept of managing one's finances.

If you enjoy her work, please leave a review on either amazon.com or goodreads.com. Or, send via email to: admin@kendyljameson.com. Additionally, please follow the author at:

KendylJameson.com

Facebook.com/KendylJameson

Twitter.com/KendylJameson

www.ingramcontent.com/pod-product-compliance
Lightning Source LLC
Chambersburg PA
CBHW022332280326
41934CB00006B/606